MW00629190

COCKTAILS
OF ASIA

**REGIONAL RECIPES AND THE
SPIRITED STORIES BEHIND THEM**

For Tom, Beckaly, Mum and Theo, because I wouldn't be here without you believing in me. And to the entire bar industry, of course.

TABLE OF CONTENTS

DEAR READER

At the age of 16, my grandfather showed me a slideshow of his trip to South America. No one in my family really traveled except him, and I myself had only been to two countries. It was a eureka moment for me: I suddenly realized there was a world beyond London, and I had to see it.

Fast forward to the age of 23, when I packed my bags and moved to rural Thailand to teach English. That was the beginning of my love affair with Asia: the people, culture, landscape, and especially the food and drink. I've spent almost a third of my life living in the region, and my nomadic ways took me to living in Seoul, traveling the world whenever I could, and eventually settling in Hong Kong — for now.

Hong Kong's food and beverage scene is unrivaled, and I'd never experienced anything like it. Still a teacher, I used all my free time to pound the pavement in search of the best food and cocktails. I eventually landed a job as food and drink editor at Time Out Hong Kong, and it wasn't long before I became more and more ingrained in the city's F&B scene.

I gradually found myself wrestling with the morality of writing reviews — I struggled with critiquing restaurants and bars that were someone's livelihood. I saw how much heart and soul went into these venues and found myself gravitating more and more towards the bar industry, which welcomed me with open arms. For the first time, I felt like I'd found my people.

We spoke the same language, we enjoyed the same things, and everyone was so collaborative — a far cry from the often cut-throat world of journalism.

I began freelancing for bar industry trade publication DRiNK Magazine, and that was it. After a full swan dive into bardom, I also began to take up bartending shifts wherever I could, absorbing knowledge and

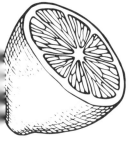

falling head over heels in love with the intricacy of spirits and cocktails. The DRiNK role became full time, and allowed me to marry my two favorite things: Asia and booze. I also bartended part-time at a bar, The Old Man in Hong Kong, which would later become globally renowned.

I genuinely love advocating for and celebrating Asia's bar industry. I've never met such a talented group of individuals who remain humble yet work so hard and collaborate to achieve their goals, making my work and passion even more enjoyable, and eventually leading me to what I never thought possible: writing this book.

This book is by no means exhaustive, but serves as a love letter to the bar industry and the driving forces — the people and the places — behind it. Thank you for everything you do and for the beautiful recipes that grace this book. Cheers.

Holly Graham

Author

A MOVEABLE FEAST

by Agung Prabowo for Penicillin, Hong Kong

Agung Prabowo is a multi-award winning bartender behind several venues in Hong Kong. Favoring a career in hospitality over continuing further studies, Agung began his foray into the industry as a busboy in his native Jakarta. He eventually scored a role at the Mandarin Oriental Jakarta, and when the hotel moved him to Hong Kong to help with opening in 2005, he began to carve out a name for himself.

It was when Agung joined The Lobster Bar at the Island Shangri-La hotel that things really took off. He was renowned for hosting wild nights of hedonism, where he'd often be seen standing on the bar top pouring whisky down the throats of eager guests. In 2017, Agung teamed up with fellow hospitality stalwarts Roman Ghale and James Tamang, and the trio opened Ernest Hemingway-themed bar The Old Man. The bar skyrocketed to global acclaim, winning the best bar in Asia at Asia's 50 Best Bars 2019.

With its use of equipment such as rotary evaporators, unusual ingredients like redistilled sea water, and a unique capital I-shaped bar with a chilled strip down the middle to keep cocktails

cold, the bar was the first of its kind. The group later expanded to Singapore to open another spot. I was fortunate to have had a stint working at The Old Man, and my time there was instrumental to expanding my bartending and hospitality skills.

While Agung and team enjoyed immense success with The Old Man, all good things must come to an end, and Agung and Roman left to join forces with their wives Laura and Katy, opening two new concepts in 2020. DEAD& — pronounced "dead end" — is located in Hong Kong's party district of Lan Kwai Fong and has a rowdy, peanut-shells-on-the-sticky-floor kind of vibe, with cheap drinks, boozy slushies and an anything goes mentality.

The antithesis of this is the city's first closed loop bar: Penicillin. Taking its name from the antibiotic, this lab-like bar melds Agung's love for experimental cocktails with fermentation methods, while putting sustainability at the forefront. Agung drew inspiration from groundbreaking restaurant NOMA in Copenhagen, showcasing local ingredients as well as upcycling "waste" from neighboring restaurants.

A Moveable Feast

This cocktail takes its name from the Ernest Hemingway book that documents his years as a struggling expat journalist and writer in Paris during the 1920s. Back in those days, Hemingway and fellow writers loved to go to Harry's New York Bar in Paris and drink their famous Bloody Mary. A Moveable Feast is a twist on this, with a clarified version topped with a briney oyster leaf.

37.5ml	ecoSPIRITS T&T Vodka distilled with clams*
45ml	clarified spiced cherry tomato**
22.5ml	clear salted coconut syrup***
15ml	clarified lemon juice****

Method

1. Infuse the cocktail in a cheese wax-coated bottle***** for 24 hours.
2. Keep chilled and pour straight into a rocks glass over a large ice block.

Garnish

Oyster leaf

*ecoSPIRITS T&T Vodka distilled with clams

350g fresh clams; 150ml sea water; 50g sea salt; 50g kosher salt; 750ml ecoSPIRITS T&T Vodka

Blend all ingredients in heavy-duty blender to break up shells. Place mix in rotary evaporator flask until original liquid has evaporated using these settings: temperature: 50° C; rotation: 85rpm; pressure: 120mbar; condenser temperature: -10° C; cut ABV to 40%.

**Clarified spiced cherry tomato

1l cherry tomato juice; 20g sea salt; 5g celery salt; 35ml Tabasco sauce; 35ml worchester sauce; 2bsp/l pectinex ultra SP-L; 1bsp/l chitosan; 1bsp/l kieselsol

Blend all ingredients except pectinex, chitosan and kieselsol in heavy-duty blender at medium speed until dissolved. Mix liquid and enzymes in jug and set aside for 5min. Place liquid in centrifuge bucket evenly and spin at 4000rpm for 30min. Strain and bottle.

***Clear salted coconut syrup

1l fresh coconut water; 750g sugar; 2bsp sea salt; 1bsp Arabic gum

Blend all ingredients in Thermomix blender on medium speed until sugar dissolves. Strain and bottle.

****Clarified lemon juice

1l lemon juice; 2g pectinex ultra SP L2; 2g chitosan; 4g kieselsol; 20g citric acid; 20g malic acid

Add pectinex and kieselsol to lemon juice and stir. Cover and allow to sit for 15min. Add 2g of chitosan and stir. Cover and leave for 15min. Add 2g more of kieselsol and stir. Place mixture into centrifuge and spin for 25min at high speed. Add citric acid solution (20g citric acid and 80ml filtered water) and malic acid solution (20g malic acid and 80ml filtered water).

*****Cheese wax-coated bottle

Heat cheese wax of your choice in jug immersed in bain-marie. While wax is still hot, pour some into glass bottle and roll hot wax around to coat inside of bottle. Pour cocktail into bottle and leave to infuse in fridge for 24hrs or longer.

ANTING ANTING NI MALVAR

by Kalel Demetrio for Agimat Foraging Bar and Kitchen, Manila

A gimat is the Tagalog word for a talisman instilled with powers to protect the person bearing it from different forces, and the bearer in this tale is Kalel Demetrio.

His bar, Agimat, focuses on the provinces of the Philippines, on a rotating basis, and a vast majority of the menu uses ingredients from the area. Take for example, southern province Batangas on the coast, which is home to various cultures, and features rich produce from the ocean, highlands and uplands.

Kalel travels around each province under the guidance of local historians and shamans who imbue their knowledge of the unfamiliar produce — which is something he advocates for, as well as the farmers of these local ingredients. The menu is divided into five elements: fire, water, land, air and life. Water drinks feature carbonated liquids such as homemade spritzes or tonics. Drinks under the fire section are prepared using fire, such as grilling and boiling; fire is also part of the final presentation.

Cocktails in the gas section feature liquid nitrogen and smoking guns, while earth drinks use foraged produce. As for the life section? That's where Kalel presents his love for all the ingredients, with zero restrictions. Kalel also creates a lot of fermented beverages, such as shrubs, vinegars, kombucha and mead, which feature heavily in Agimat's non-alcoholic offerings.

The cocktail Anting Anting Ni Malvar, meaning "talisman of General Miguel Malvar", is inspired by Batangas province. "In Batangas, there is a municipality called Malvar, named after one of the greatest revolutionary generals of the Philippines," explains Kalel. "He served in the Philippine Revolution and the Philippine-American War, and legend has it he evaded danger through a talisman — hence why he always dominated the battlefield and was never captured."

Kalel says Malvar Batangas is abundant with produce, and its elevation of almost 400 meters above sea level means there are lots of bodies of water, such as volcanic lakes. "It's also the home of Taal volcano, and the surrounding soil is rich with the sulfuric and mineral content from the volcano. I designed this cocktail based on all the produce from Malvar, and it has become one of the most iconic cocktails at Agimat listed in the air section," shares Kalel.

Anting Anting Ni Malvar

This iconic Agimat cocktail uses produce from Malvar in the Batangas province of the Philippines.

45ml	gin
45ml	dalandan citrus juice
½bsp	jigsaw pepper wild honey*
20ml	rosemary syrup**
20ml	vodka
2g	fresh turmeric and ginger
1 drop	saline solution^

Method
1. Slightly muddle the turmeric and ginger with the dalandan citrus juice in one tin.
2. Add the other ingredients and ice and shake vigorously.
3. Fine strain into a coupe glass.

Garnish
Dehydrated dalandan citrus, burnt rosemary and dehydrated rose petals

*Jigsaw pepper honey (or any spicy pepper)
5-10g pepper; 150ml sugar cane vinegar; 1l honey
Blend peppers with sugar cane vinegar. Cook and bring to boil, then let cool down. Blend with 1l honey and store at room temperature.

**Rosemary syrup
30g rosemary sprigs; 1l water; 1kg white sugar
Blend rosemary sprigs in water. Boil the mixture, then strain off sprigs. Add sugar and stir until dissolved, then refrigerate.

ATLAS FRENCH 75

by Jesse Vida for ATLAS, Singapore

No trip to Singapore is complete without a visit to gawp at the sheer beauty of ATLAS. This monolithic shrine to gin is the glamorous palace that Gatsby wishes he could have thrown parties in. The bar is housed in the ground level of the Art Deco tower Parkview Square, a building that wouldn't look out of place in Gotham City.

ATLAS's spirits collection of over 1,550 bottles is housed in the bar's masterpiece: a stunning eight-meter tower located in the center of the space. Of those bottles, more than 1,300 are an ever-changing rotation of gins from all over the world. Staff access the bottles using a ladder in the tower, and the mirrors behind the bottles are doors that open from the inside.

The team is led by dapper gent and head bartender Jesse Vida, and fierce assistant head bartender and resident gin researcher Yana Kamaruddin, a pair who are deeply knowledgeable and passionate about gin. Jesse and Yana, along with bar admin manager Lauren Sosnowsky, who is in charge of gin procurement, hold monthly Juniper Society meetings, where members are introduced to new gins through tastings and guest speakers.

ATLAS Martini

ATLAS doesn't use many Asian ingredients in its cocktails, preferring to stick to strict European guidelines — given the bar is an ode to 1920s European hotel lobbies. However, the gin collection does feature bottles from all over the region, including Cambodia, China, Japan, Singapore and Thailand, to name a few. ATLAS also specializes in Champagne, with more than 250 labels on offer.

Of course, no bar specializing in gin would be complete without its own signature martini, and the ATLAS Martini features London dry gin, blanc vermouth, orange bitters and Champagne vinegar. However, it's the ATLAS French 75 that marries the bar's championing of gin and Champagne. The cocktail sprung to mind while Jesse was first interviewing for ATLAS. "As soon as I learned the two pillars of the ATLAS beverage program were gin and Champagne, I knew we needed to have our own French 75. I didn't want to veer too far from the original, but added peach liqueur because peach and Champagne is a no-brainer flavor pairing; and a touch of salt because salt makes everything better! We also pour it tableside to give it a more experiential aspect."

ATLAS French 75

This is ATLAS's take on the classic French 75, originally created by Harry MacElhone in 1915 at Harry's New York bar in Paris.

1 dash	saline solution^
20ml	lemon
15ml	1:1 sugar syrup^
10ml	creme de peche
40ml	Citadelle Original Gin
20ml	Champagne

Method
1. Put all ingredients except Champagne into tins with ice, and shake.
2. Strain into a Champagne flute.
3. Top with Champagne.

Garnish
Candied kumquat

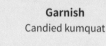

BAK KWA
MANHATTAN

by Jay Gray for Sago House, Singapore

Jay Gray (left); Desiree Silva; and George C. Abhishek

B orn in the midst of the pandemic, Sago House is a bar by ex-whisky brand ambassador Jay Gray, Singapore hospitality stalwart Desiree Silva, and Spiffy Dapper owner George C. Abhishek.

The trio quite literally poured blood, sweat and tears into this bar built almost entirely by their own hands, with little cash and no investors. All three were still working full-time jobs during the build, using any spare time to hammer away, lay bricks and tiles, and wire the bar using skills learned from online tutorials.

Located in an old Singaporean shophouse, the bar is fitted out with upcycled textiles such as coffee bean sacks — used to upholster seating at the bar — and items salvaged from closing venues. The result is an eclectic space that pays homage to its Southeast Asian roots, highlighting features such as the shophouses' original green stained-glass windows.

Sago House avoids being conceptualized, drawing instead from experience that Jay, Desiree and George have collected during their years in hospitality, as well as all that they love about bars. The menu focuses on six classic cocktail styles: martinis, sidecars, old fashioneds, highballs, flips, and sours — using different flavors to create a drink in each category on a weekly rotating basis. This also allows the bar to showcase an ever-changing list of different spirits brands.

While the menu changes, there is a core "secret menu" that remains, and the team has been kind enough to share one of its recipes, the Bak Kwa Manhattan, in this book.

Bak Kwa Manhattan

This is Sago House's take on the classic Manhattan, featuring bak kwa (a Fujian-style sweet pork jerky) infused in bourbon.

50ml	bak kwa bourbon*
25ml	chipotle torino mix**
2.5ml	cherry liqueur
2.5ml	Cointreau
10ml	water
1 spritz	chocolate bitters

Method
1. Put all ingredients into a bottle and chill in the fridge.
2. Pour into a coupe glass.
3. Spritz chocolate bitters on top.

*Bak kwa bourbon
700ml bourbon; 500g bak kwa
Combine bourbon and bak kwa in sous vide bag. Sous vide at 40° C
for 2hrs. Filter and place in freezer
for 4-6hrs. Strain until clear.

**Chipotle torino mix
450ml rosso vermouth; 200ml Punt e Mes; 50ml Cynar; 10g dried chipotle
Blend liquid ingredients together in sous vide bag. Add dried chipotle. Sous vide at 40° C for 2hrs. Strain and bottle.

BAMBOO

The Meiji Restoration of 1868 marked a period in Japan when feudalism came to an end, and Japan's modernization got underway — opening the country up to the rest of the world. South of Tokyo, sleepy fishing village Yokohama became a gateway for the west, and it was where Japan saw its first railway, electrical grid and brewery.

It was also a gateway for cocktails, via bartenders like German Louis Eppinger, who had previously tended bar in San Francisco. In 1889, Eppinger arrived in Yokohama and joined the Grand Hotel as bar manager, where he was renowned for his skills in cocktail creation and hospitality. He worked at the hotel until he died in 1908.

Eppinger is also credited with inventing the Bamboo cocktail, a simple blend of sherry and dry vermouth — which is a twist on the Adonis, consisting of fino sherry and sweet vermouth. The Bamboo became the hotel's house specialty.

The Bamboo was also Japan's first cocktail export to America, where it became popular in California. William Boothby's 1908 book, *The World's Drinks and How to Mix Them*, is the first written record of the drink, detailed as equal parts sherry and dry vermouth, with two dashes of orange bitters, a twist of lemon and an olive.

Nowadays, the proportions and the inclusion of a garnish are up for debate, but the cocktail remains popular in Japan, where bartenders use more sherry to create a drier cocktail. While the drink is traditionally stirred, some Japanese bartenders prefer to use a technique called rolling, where the drink is poured back and forth between the two parts of a tin, allowing the drink to aerate.

Like much cocktail legend and lore, this story is widely accepted, but cocktail blog *Everythinginthebar* throws a spanner in the works, as it reveals that the first written evidence of the Bamboo was actually in 1886, which was three years before Eppinger moved to Japan. Of course, Eppinger could have created this cocktail while working in San Francisco, but newspaper *Western Kansas World* credits a drink of three parts sherry and one part vermouth called the Bamboo to an Englishman. Allegedly, a similar article appeared in another newspaper eight days later, crediting the mystery Englishman but adding that the drink may have taken its name from the fact that once it's consumed, the drinker feels like "raising Cain."

While lots of cocktail history is lost in drunken conversations that travel the globe, whether Eppinger was the original creator of the Bamboo or not, he created hype around the drink that is still popular today and is arguably one of Japan's most historic cocktails.

Bamboo

Eppinger's classic recipe, supposedly invented in Japan, never states the kind of sherry used. This means the character of the drink has the potential to be customized, using different types of sherries.

60ml	dry vermouth
20ml	sherry
2 dashes	orange bitters

Method
1. Place all ingredients into a mixing glass with ice and stir until chilled. Alternatively, roll liquid between tins.

2. Strain into a Martini glass.

BAN BAN GIBSON

by Holly Graham

While being asked to choose my favorite cocktail always proves a challenging task, if you were to hold a gun to my head, I would tell you it's a gin Gibson — a martini-style drink that uses a pickled onion in place of an olive or lemon twist. I'm a real sucker for pickles, thanks to my Eastern European and Jewish heritage — so for me, a Gibson is the best way to jazz up a martini.

I love martinis in general, which is curious since I never had myself down as a gin lover, preferring agave spirits or whisk(e)y instead. However, I began to realize that it was gin and tonic I wasn't the biggest fan of. A martini is a fantastic way to showcase a gin, and when my husband and I built a bar in our home — a wild moment in the midst of the COVID-19 pandemic — we began to play with classics like Gibsons a lot more, and customized them to our liking.

A Gin from Hanoi

Founded by Daniel Nguyen, Sông Cái Distillery is based in Vietnam's capital of Hanoi. Nguyen returned to Vietnam to work on sustainable development, highland agroforestry and ethnobotany projects. He was based in remote mountainous villages, where he worked with minority tribes and learned about the terroir and botany intersected with culture and community through foraging botanicals. Nguyen became immersed in regional food, spirits and flavors, and Sông Cái Distillery continues to work with these communities to source botanicals.

Sông Cái Distillery's range of Vietnam gins feature a variety of heirloom and native botanicals unique to the different regions of Vietnam. The Việt Nam Floral Gin pays homage to deltaic flower culture and includes hoàng lan (cananga odorata or ylang-ylang); jasmine; ngọc lan (michelia alba); pomelo blossom; and móng rồng (artabotrys hexapetalus).

The flagship Việt Nam Dry Gin focuses on highland botanicals including mắc mật (clausena indica) fruit and leaf; đia siêu (ficus) wood; mắc khén (zanthoxylum rhetsa); coriander seed; and cassia.

Nose: Jasmine with a slight hint of vanilla, mint and chamomile — for an overall fresh and clean aroma.

Palate: Mellow floral notes of jasmine, marigold and chamomile. No sharp citrus, just soft vegetal notes and a creamy mouthfeel.

As a pickled onion fiend, I prefer my Gibsons to really taste of them, while not masking the gin. It's a tough task, as it really depends on the onions and gin used. I'd get strange looks at the bars when I ordered my Gibson with extra pickled onion vinegar, and usually found that it still wasn't enough. I decided to refer to these drinks as "dirty Gibsons", and friends would often go in for a curious sip — only to be pleasantly surprised that my palate wasn't absolutely bonkers.

When the Sông Cái team sent me their gin, and Summer Lo of ARGO kindly gifted me homemade pickled onions one Christmas, I knew it was time to experiment again. Sông Cái's Dry Gin stood up against my excessive love for pickled onions, creating a Gibson laden with umami. And there it was: the perfect dirty — or ban ban, which means dirty in Vietnamese — Gibson.

This drink will often find its way into the hands of my friends towards the end of a gathering at my home, and it always goes down well. But if you don't like pickled onions, I'm afraid I just can't help you there!

Ban Ban Gibson

The Ban Ban Gibson is a martini variation with a generous helping of pickled onion vinegar.

60ml	Sông Cái Dry Gin
10ml	bianco vermouth
3 bsp	onion vinegar

Method
1. Stir all ingredients with ice until chilled.
2. Strain into a coupe glass over a pickled onion.

BANANA NEGRONI

by the team at The Daily Tot, Hong Kong

Hong Kong rum bar The Daily Tot takes its name from a 300-year-old Royal Navy tradition. At the strike of noon, sailors used to throw back a 70-millimeter "tot" of rum for warmth, camaraderie and a dash of Dutch courage. The hefty measure was later reduced to 30 millimeters, as 70 millimeters understandably made for more sozzled sailors. Clearly not a very healthy habit, the daily tot tradition ended on July 31, 1970, which became known as Black Tot Day.

Owner Tiana Ludhani was raised in Barbados, and wanted to share the drinking culture of not only the Caribbean, but of the sailors, by serving a tot of daily-changing rum, as well as a range of cocktails celebrating the category. The Daily Tot also nods to Cuba through its cigar collection and its sobremesa vibe: the Cuban tradition of having a relaxed rum and cigar after dinner.

Tiana recommends drinking rum with a ginger beer or coconut water chaser; or sampling the daily tot, which will be mixed with anything that best opens up the rum, from soda to lime juice. While The Daily Tot showcases various rum flights, it doesn't strive to boast Asia's largest rum collection, preferring to focus on Caribbean and European rums that are great for sipping and have a story behind them.

Cocktails here steer away from typical rum drinks, but that's not to say the team won't whip you up a mean mojito or pina colada if you so desire. Think classics that use a variety of rums for the base, such as rum old fashioneds and rum Negronis.

The bar opened smack bang in the middle of 2020, when COVID-19 restrictions were particularly tight for F&B venues in Hong Kong, and watching the team achieve success in the face of adversity restored hope that Hong Kong's bar industry would not be completely decimated by the pandemic.

Banana Negroni

Tiana wanted to see how far The Daily Tot could push a classic Negroni, and discovered Campari works really well with very ripe bananas. This twist on the classic focuses on the rum, with the added sweetness of banana.

45ml	Flor De Cãna 7 Years infused with banana*
25ml	Campari
15ml	sweet vermouth

Method
1. Put all ingredients into a mixing glass with ice and stir.
2. Strain into a chilled rocks glass with cubed ice.

Garnish
Slice of caramelized fresh banana

*Flor De Cãna 7 Years infused with banana
1 bottle Flor De Cãna 7 Years; 200g overly ripened banana; 1bsp banana extract; 1bsp pectinex

Mix all ingredients in container and hand blend. Place in centrifuge at 4000rpm for 15min to clarify. If centrifuge not available, infuse ingredients overnight and strain.

BATAVIA MILK PUNCH

by Kiki Moka for The Cocktail Club, Jakarta

Upon graduating high school, drummer Kiki Moka hung up his sticks and took a job as a bar back at the Batavia Cafe in Jakarta. Like many bartenders, Kiki was wooed by the job after watching the classic film, *Cocktail*, starring Tom Cruise, but still remains a rockstar at heart.

Starting off washing glasses, eventually Kiki learned the classics and became a flair bartender, forgetting everything he knew about executing a well-made cocktail. Under the mentorship of a few

Sweet Flavors of Asia

While Monin started out in France, the gourmet syrup brand has production facilities all over the world, including in Asian countries like China and Malaysia, and it also offers a range of flavors using Asian ingredients. Le Sirop de Monin Pandan uses the tropical plant to create an emerald green syrup with vegetal hints rounded by a vanilla and coconut-like flavor. Le Sirop de Monin Purple Sweet Potato can be used in both sweet and savory drinks, and is an ingredient popular in Japanese and Filipino snacks. Le Sirop de Monin Osmanthus is derived from the flowering plant that is popular in Chinese cuisine and medicine for its detoxifying qualities.

Hong Kong personalities — including fellow Indonesian Agung Prabowo, co-founder of Penicillin — he refreshed his knowledge of classics, and joined cocktail competition Diageo World Class in 2011. He got through to the global finals, and credits the experience with shaping the bartender he is today.

Kiki is undoubtedly one of the first people to spring to mind when it comes to the bar scene in Jakarta. His love for travel and his penchant for sharing acquired knowledge with fellow Indonesian bartenders arguably makes him a pioneer of the capital's bar scene. He joined The Union Group in 2012, having worked with one of the founders for nine years prior, and now looks after the group's 16 bars as the head mixologist.

In 2021, Kiki and his team opened their dream bar, The Cocktail Club. The bar is run entirely by bartenders, serving unique drinks featuring local ingredients, inventive techniques and unusual flavor combinations. Ingredients include Indonesian spirit arrack, citrus fruit calamansi and fermented cempedak: a fruit similar to jackfruit. Of course there are classics, but the team has added Asian twists to them. Take for instance the Irish Coffee, which uses gula melaka, a type of palm sugar used in Southeast Asia, as the sweetener.

Kiki says The Cocktail Club is special, as it's the group's first real cocktail bar. "We can finally focus on serving craft cocktails and curated whiskies, instead of having to also produce non-alcoholic drinks required in our other all-day establishments. Aside from that, we also have a stake in it, which makes it really special for us, and the whole bar is run by bartenders. Every single member of the team can make your cocktails."

Kiki wants The Cocktail Club to be a bar that takes its drinks seriously, but is still fun. "A guest can experience well-made cocktails or rare single malts in a plush environment, with great music, but they don't have to speak in hushed tones or dress up stiffly. We want everyone to feel welcome and have a good time."

The Cocktail Club also features a project called Traveling Whisky, born in the COVID-19 pandemic to allow whisky lovers of Jakarta a sense of community. A bottle is passed around, and the recipient must pour a shot for themselves, then add back the equivalent amount of their chosen whisk(e)y before passing it onto the next person.

I feel like the Traveling Whisky is Kiki personified in a boozy idea. He's all about family, community and sharing. I have incredibly fond memories of a Hong Kong takeover he organized across his group's bars in Jakarta. Some of Hong Kong's bar owners and tenders flew in to do guest bartending shifts for a few days — including myself while working at The Old Man. While the trip was a blur of incredible food, late nights and tequila shots, it was one of the most fun trips I took as a bartender. After my shift, sweaty and tipsy, Kiki announced he was treating us all to tattoos, and I got The Old Man's logo inked on my arm at 2am at the bar.

The trip culminated in all of the Hong Kong bars taking over country club Cork & Screw, and the night finished with us all jumping in the pool fully clothed. Long story short, I woke up soaking wet, with 10 minutes to spare before our transport to the airport. That was one hell of a flight home!

Batavia Milk Punch

Kiki's drink is a cross between a classic milk punch and the 19th-century cocktail Batavia Punch. This modern take celebrates Kiki's love for arrack and the city of Batavia, or present-day Jakarta.

Yield: 10 portions

200ml	Batavia arrack	60ml	Galliano
100ml	spiced rum	200ml	cold-pressed pineapple juice
500ml	fresh milk		
75ml	Monin Strawberry Syrup	10g	milk oolong tea leaves
		100ml	calamansi juice

Method

1. Mix all items except for milk, Monin Strawberry Syrup and milk oolong tea leaves.

2. Mix milk and Monin Strawberry Syrup together and heat over steam. Pour strawberry milk into the rest of the mixture. Slowly stir for 10 seconds until strawberry milk splits. Let stand for 30 minutes and strain through cheesecloth.

3. Once milk punch has clarified, use bain-marie method to infuse the milk oolong tea leaves.

4. Brew for 5 minutes to desired flavor, then strain.

5. Leave to cool, then pour into Gruyere-waxed empty bottle* and store in the fridge.

To Serve

1. Pour 75ml of the Batavia Milk Punch into mixing glass and stir with ice.

2. Strain into a tumbler over an ice block.

Garnish

Slice of Gruyere cheese

*Gruyere-waxed bottle

100g Gruyere cheese; 25g bee's wax
Heat Gruyere cheese and bee's wax in a bain-marie until melted and mixed. Pour into empty 750ml bottle, seal and roll bottle so liquid coats the entire inside of bottle.

WHAT IS
BATAVIA ARRACK?

ACEH

SUMATERA
UTARA

SUMATERA
BARAT

JAMBI

KEPULAUAN
BELITUNG

BENGKULU

LAMPUNG

BANTEN

JAWA
BARAT

YOGYAKARTA

JAKARTA

JAWA TIMUR

TE

KALIM
TIM

KALIMANTAN
BARAT

KALIMANTAN
TENGAH

KALI
SE

While arrack is a broad Hindi phrase for Asian spirits made from flowers, nuts, fruits, cane or a mixture of the ingredients, Batavia arrack is specifically made from fermenting and distilling sugar cane molasses and red rice. Batavia arrack is a molasses-based sugar cane distillate similar to rum — however, it predates rum and is often considered one of the oldest spirits in the world. What makes Batavia arrack different is the traditional inclusion of red rice in the fermentation. Dried rice is malted and turned into a cake, then added to the molasses along with a local yeast for a long and slow fermentation followed by double-pot distillation and a short maturation in teak wood.

SULAWESI TENGAH

MALUKU UTARA

PAPUA

INDONESIA

AWESI LATAN

SULAWESI TENGGARA

A

NUSATENGGARA TIMUR

Batavia takes its name from Indonesia's capital during Dutch colonialism in the 17th century; it is now known as Jakarta. Batavia arrack made its way to the west via European trade routes with Indonesia from the mid-17th to 19th centuries. The spirit became popular, commanded a high price on menus across Europe and the Americas, and was commonly used in punches — which predate the cocktail — mixed with sugar, teas, citrus and other flavorings. As rum production grew in the 1800s, it became cheaper to produce and to drink, so consumption of the spirit skyrocketed, and its popularity increased.

Author David Wondrich's book, *Punch,* features many recipes including Batavia arrack, as it's the original alcoholic base ingredient for punches. He has also written in-depth articles for *The Daily Beast* detailing the history of how Batavia arrack came to be, for those wanting a history lesson dating as far back as the 1500s.

Batavia arrack, for want of a better word, is a funky spirit, with a strong, musky aroma. As it is considered a precursor to the global rum category, one should play around with it in traditional rum cocktails and highballs, or use it to add depth to cocktails along with other spirits.

BE HUMBLE PEACHES

by Vu Ngoc for Doozy, Hanoi

Vu Ngoc

ounded by Vietnamese bar veteran Vu Ngoc, Doozy, in Vietnam's capital of Hanoi, is both high-tech and minimalist. Signature cocktails at Doozy use lots of local ingredients that are prepared with equipment considered unchartered territory in Vietnam's bar scene, like rotary evaporators and centrifuges.

After graduating in marketing, Vu began bartending in 2012 and credits an eye-opening trip to Shanghai for inspiring him to open his own bar. This is where I first met Vu, and I loved his cheeky personality and thoughtful drinks.

Bartender-owned bars are still relatively new in Vietnam, and Doozy is one of the trailblazers. Originally from Ho Chi Minh City, Vu moved to Hanoi, romanced by the slower pace of life, local culture and diversity of cuisine, thanks to the north's rich local ingredients.

Vu decided to make Doozy a marriage of what he calls the classic north and the lively south. "Like me being born in the south and moving north, Doozy is born in a completely different way to other Vietnamese bars in terms of brand, characteristics and products," he explains.

Hidden behind an eyewear store, Doozy's stainless steel-and-brick wall decor also boasts a bar top perfect for displaying the bar's equipment, ingredients and skills. Of course, Doozy means something outstanding or unique of its kind, and here the music, hospitality, vibe and cocktails are both unique and outstanding.

Cocktails at Doozy draw inspiration from seasonal ingredients and local products, using the bar's equipment to extract the flavors and showcase them to the max. Signature drinks such as Call Me Doozy is a twist on the classic Boulevardier with whisky, banana, strawberry and mango vinegar, using local fruits. Be Humble Peaches even goes as far as using locally made spirits, such as Sông Cái Dry Gin.

Be Humble Peaches

This cocktail was inspired by seasonal and local fruits in Hanoi. A little acidity from local apricots balances the sweetness and creaminess from the cheese and vermouth, and also bolsters the citrus and herbal notes of the gin.

45ml	Sông Cái Dry Gin
30ml	Vietnamese salted apricot cordial*
20ml	peach and cheddar vermouth**

Method
1. Put all ingredients and ice into a shaker and shake.
2. Strain into a rocks glass.

Garnish
Dried apricot

*Vietnamese salted apricot cordial
500g apricot; 10g salt; 1l water;
15g citric acid; 10g lactic acid
Put all ingredients except acids in cooking pot. Cook all ingredients for 30min. Let liquid rest for 30min. Add acid and stir until dissolved.

**Peach and cheddar vermouth
700ml bianco sweet vermouth; 200g fresh peach; 100g cheddar cheese; 5g lactic acid
Blend all ingredients except acid. Let liquid rest for 10min. Add acid and stir until dissolved. Cold-infuse for 48hrs, then strain.

BOURBON STREET

by Yangdup Lama for Sidecar, New Delhi

Minakshi Singh, co-founder of cocktail bars Sidecar plus Cocktails and Dreams Speakeasy in India, is something of a trailblazer. Minakshi began bartending after graduating, falling in love with hospitality and cocktails. She's a trailblazer, because there aren't that many women behind the stick in India, and this was especially true when she first started out. Sidecar is also often credited for putting India on the global cocktail map.

Minakshi's parents had a tough time grasping why she wanted to bartend, especially as just a few years before Minakshi embarked on her career, a model serving drinks at a party in New Delhi was murdered, and it shook the community. Jessica Lal was shot

Yangdup Lama

Minakshi (second from left); Yangdup (center); and team

dead for not serving a man who wanted to get drinks after closing, and Minakshi says this set back bartending as a credible job even further. While things are improving, Minakshi says there's still a ways to go, but her achievements are a testament to her, and to India's growing bar scene.

In 2003, Minakshi met her now-business partner and lauded bartender Yangdup Lama, who helped steer her career towards beverage consulting and training. She and Yangdup eventually decided to open a bar in 2012, and Cocktails and Dreams Speakeasy was born.

The classic cocktails that seem ten a penny now, such as Negronis and old fashioneds, were a hard sell when they opened, but with more people traveling, international bartenders passing through, and knowledge building, guests soon came to love the bar. So much so, Minakshi and Yangdup decided to

open their dream bar, Sidecar. The hidden spot is where Minakshi says the pair did exactly what they wanted to do: showcase their skills, focus on sustainability and make lots of ingredients in-house.

It was 2020 when Sidecar made an international breakthrough. The bar was the only Indian bar on Asia's 50 Best Bars list that year, and only the second bar from India to ever rank on the list. The following year, the bar took it up a notch and came in at 47 on The World's 50 Best Bars list — the first time a bar from India had featured since 2010.

Minakshi, who admits she previously took more of a background role, preferring to let Yangdup and the other bartenders shine, has decided to now use her voice for the greater good. Her mission is to show women that working in bars is a viable career choice, and she encourages more to join the industry.

A memorable nugget of wisdom Minakshi shared with me regarding hospitality, is that cocktails can be fixed if they're not right — but service can't be reissued if you mess it up. She's clearly very dedicated to the craft of hospitality, and in the age of fangled cocktail technology and techniques, it's a rare yet very important thing indeed. When people talk about the ascent of India's bar scene, Minakshi and Yangdup's names will definitely be the first to be mentioned.

Bourbon Street

In 1975, American writer Walker Percy wrote a famous essay for *Esquire*, simply called "Bourbon." Percy loved his corn whiskey, and this cocktail pays tribute to his favorite drink.

45ml	bourbon whiskey
25ml	Sidecar raisin sherry*
15ml	Campari

Method
1. Stir all ingredients in a mixing glass with ice.
2. Strain and serve in a rocks glass over ice.

Garnish
Orange peel

*Sidecar raisin sherry
Age cabernet sauvignon in an ex-bourbon cask for 3mos. Sweeten with raisins.

CACTUS

by the team at Analogue, Singapore

O pened in 2021, Analogue is the second venue by Vijay Mudaliar, the sustainability expert behind game-changing Native. Vijay is known for his eco-conscious approach to bartending, and Analogue — taking its name from the dictionary definition of a person or thing seen as comparable to another — takes his ethos to the next level.

Frustrated with the idea of luxury leaning towards expensive and unsustainable ingredients such as foie gras and wagyu, the bar uses more environmentally friendly analogues for overfarmed products and considers alternatives for ingredients at risk from climate change. Ingredients on Analogue's cocktail menu include: carob instead of chocolate; chicory instead of coffee; and tonka bean instead of vanilla; as their flavors are comparable and not nearly as overfarmed. It also follows that the food offerings at Analogue are vegan- and vegetarian-friendly.

Analogue showcases the potential ingredients of tomorrow, such as cacti and succulents, as they need little water and will thrive under the planet's ever-increasing temperatures and subsequent droughts; and the algae spirulina, which can also be used to create clean energy. Refined sugar is also omitted from the bar, with sweeteners such as xylitol and monk fruit used instead.

With the rise of mindful drinking, Analogue features a section of non-alcoholic cocktails. To create these, Vijay took inspiration from perfumes and uses edible essential oils, hydrosols, vegan honey and fermented drinks such as kombuchas to bolster Analogue's booze-free offerings.

The venue is designed with sustainability in mind, featuring a 3D-printed bar top made from 1,600 kilograms' worth of recycled plastic (part of which is lowered for wheelchair accessibility) as well as tables made of mushrooms.

Cactus

A homage to the robust succulent and cacti families created by R&D lead Nicholas Leong, Cactus uses ingredients from these plant families to showcase their versatility and potential usage as an "ingredient of tomorrow".

500g	mezcal vida
100g	lime distillate*
250g	pink dragonfruit
250g	prickly pear
150g	aloe vera
100g	tartaric solution
100g	malic acid
150g	pasilla reduction**

Method
1. Blend all ingredients and clarify through centrifuge at 4000rpm for 20 minutes. Strain through a cheesecloth. Yield is approximately 90%.
2. Shake 120ml of the mixture with ice and strain into a coupette glass.

Garnish
Tajin salt sim

*Lime distillate
300g limes; 1l vodka
Blend limes and vodka with a hand blender and send through the rotary evaporator at 55° C, 80rpm, 20mbar.

**Pasilla Reduction
15g pasilla chilis; 500g xylitol; 500g water
Blend, strain and simmer in pot. Chill and bottle for use later.

CHA CHAAN
TENG HIGHBALL

by Arkadiusz Rybak for DarkSide, Hong Kong

Arkadiusz Rybak (second row, third from right)

D arkSide takes its name from both the colloquial moniker for Hong Kong's Kowloon side — where the bar is located — and its focus on all things dark. Think rare spirits such as exclusive casks of Grande Champagne cognac aged in oak or single harvest tawny port from 1994; fortified wines; amaros; and an array of chocolate and vintage cigars.

Sultry jazz and live music punctuate this elegant venue at the Rosewood hotel, which serves up classics with sustainability at the forefront — a cause that beverage director Arkadiusz Rybak is extremely passionate about. The bar's creative menus have previously featured cocktails inspired by the eight phases of the moon, an extremely interactive menu accompanied by a hologram video and a custom magic eight ball, which upon shaking, reveals the cocktail you should choose.

In a city where very few alcohol products are made locally due to a lack of space, DarkSide produced a local amaro using foraged botanicals native to Hong Kong in a first for the SAR, and one of the first for Asia. The result: Hunter in the Dark Amaro, a collaboration with spirits brand Fernet Hunter and local foraging expert Wanda Huang. The amaro is a culmination of Arkadiusz's desire to create a product that showcases the culture, produce and flavors of Hong Kong — which, unbeknownst to many, is almost 40 percent national park by landmass.

Arkadiusz and Wanda had been on foraging trips together before, and I've also been lucky enough to join on a few occasions. I've always been astounded by the incredible produce that surrounded us. Arkadiusz, meanwhile, began thinking about how the foraged ingredients could go beyond cocktails.

The DarkSide and Fernet Hunter teams sourced ingredients from Yi O Farm on the rural island of Lantau. Taking inspiration from Traditional Chinese Medicine, something that Wanda also specializes in, the amaro's botanicals include: bur marigold leaves; Chinese mugwort; citron leaves; Cuban oregano; wild ginger seeds and leaves; calamansi; calamondin; Lantana flowers and leaves; pomelo leaves; and wild Chinese peppercorns. A locally produced rice spirit serves as the base. The result is an amaro fully produced in Hong Kong, which is bright, light and floral and best enjoyed in a highball or on ice.

Cha Chaan Teng Highball

A cha chaan teng is a Hong Kong-style cafe, selling popular dishes like the city's take on French toast and milk tea, as well as macaroni soup. Another popular style of cha chaan teng drink is the salted lemon or lime with soda. This is the inspiration behind DarkSide's highball take, using salted calamansi from local farmers.

40ml	Nikka Days
20ml	salted calamansi syrup*
Top up	soda water

Method
Build into a highball glass with ice and top up with soda water.

Garnish
Calamansi half

*Salted calamansi syrup

20g salted calamansi; 200g water; 100g caster sugar

Set sous vide to 60° C. Cut calamansi in half and put into sous vide bag with water and sugar. Seal and sous vide for 2hrs. Chill in ice bath for 20min. Double strain through a coffee filter and bottle.

CHIQUITA PEPITA

by Phil Abowd for Southside Parlor, Seoul

I left my life in Seoul, South Korea for Hong Kong, having not had a decent cocktail experience of note. I'll always lament the fact that Phil Abowd threw open the doors to Southside Parlor mere months after my departure, because it's a great spot and I definitely would've propped the bar up regularly.

Southside Parlor is arguably one of Seoul's earliest craft cocktail bars, served with a hearty dose of Southern hospitality, since Phil hails from Texas. The space is like a refined American sports bar, with an arcade game console, darts and big leather sofas, but serving up drinks far from what you'd expect at a sports bar. Phil admits it took locals a while to come around to high-end cocktails in a casual space, as most were used to the glitz and glam of the Gangnam neighborhood.

Homemade ingredients create tongue-in-cheek drinks like the Dr Pepper Negroni, with dark rum, Dr Pepper vermouth, Campari, and bubbles. Fresh juices nod to Korea's spa culture in Korean Spa Day, with Korean gin, cucumber mint, aloe and lime.

Chiquita Pepita

This is a fresh, tropical take on the margarita featuring local Korean Cheongyang green chili and pepper powder that goes into just about everything. Phil wanted to find some commonality between Korean flavors and what he was used to back in Texas.

45ml	cucumber-infused Patrón Silver Tequila*
15ml	Cointreau
45ml	verdita**
15ml	lime juice
15ml	3:1 agave syrup

Method
1. Whip shake all ingredients with four to five ice cubes.
2. Fine strain into rocks glass over ice.

Garnish
Cucumber ribbon and chili flakes

*Cucumber-infused Patrón Silver Tequila
750ml Patrón Silver Tequila; 200g cucumber (thinly sliced)
Combine ingredients into vacuum bag and sous vide at 55° C for 2hrs. Strain and bottle.

**Verdita
250ml fresh pineapple juice; 10ml lime juice; 10ml 1:1 sugar syrup^; 10g spearmint (stems and leaves); 10g coriander (stems and leaves); 5g Korean Cheongyang gochu pepper (seeds removed)
Add all ingredients into blender and blend on high speed for 20s. Strain through a filter and bottle.

The team also opened one of Korea's first sustainability-forward venues via Pocket, a tiny neighborhood bar serving draft highballs. The bar upcycles Southside Parlor's single-use ingredients, such as lemon peels and spices. The bar also features an aquaponic system, as well as a bar top made out of discarded bottle glass and seashells collected from local bars and restaurants.

Phil and his partners also have relaxed, house party-style bar High House, which serves approachable natural wines and mean tacos.

I've always admired Phil's attitude — he came blazing onto the Korean bar scene as a former teacher with little experience, and still remains strong after almost a decade running bars. He's always been a great advocate for women in bartending — still a rarity in Korea — and pushes his staff to their full potential. He's also masterful at getting you obliterated, and I've had a few hazy evenings with him end in delicious late-night Korean barbecues.

D.O.K

by Mason Park for Alice Cheongdam, Seoul

Terry Kim (center); Mason Park (second from right); and team

Terry Kim is arguably one of the founding fathers of Korea's cocktail scene. His first bar, Alice Cheongdam, is still going strong after years in the business, and Terry has now expanded his empire to include eight bars across Seoul, Busan and Jeju Island.

Terry has seen the Korean bar scene shift dramatically over the years, from basic drinks to innovative creations and more independently bartender-owned bars, and he is definitely due a lot of credit for this.

After studying hotel and tourism management and serving military service, Terry began bartending in hotels in 2006. He found the constraints of hotel red tape stifled his creativity, so he opened Alice Cheongdam, an Alice in Wonderland-inspired bar, to break the mold. The hidden bar is located down a set of stairs and behind a secret door in a flower shop, which opens up into a luxe speakeasy-style venue.

While the decor is not as quirky as you'd think — it's more swanky if anything — the Alice in Wonderland sentiment is reflected in the idea that the guests are Alice, experiencing something new at the bar. The bartenders are naturally the white rabbits, leading drinkers down the rabbit hole of cocktails.

The drinks are theatrical here. Whether they're served in rabbit-shaped ceramics, or in a box billowing with smoke, they're always a sight to behold. The menu is split into the four seasons, featuring local ingredients such as omija (Korean magnolia berry tea) and soybean paste. Dongchimi, a type of white radish kimchi usually consumed in colder months, is featured in the drink Snow Crystal, which fittingly sits in the winter section and is mixed with gin and vermouth for a martini twist.

D.O.K

D.O.K stands for Definition Of Korea. Creator Mason Park regards soybean paste as a memorable soul food ingredient, and wanted to make a cocktail that combines everything by adding Korean ingredients to American liquor.

45ml	soybean butter Maker's Mark Bourbon*
15ml	amaretto
1tbsp	maple syrup
1 dash	aromatic bitters

Method
1. Put all ingredients into a mixing glass and stir.
2. Strain into a clay pot over ice.

Garnish
Soybean cookie

*Soybean butter Maker's Mark Bourbon
750ml Maker's Mark Bourbon; 40g unsalted butter; 100g soybean paste
Melt butter over low heat. Add soybean paste and mix for 2min. Cool for 5min and pour into container with Maker's Mark Bourbon. Leave at room temperature for 4hrs, agitating occasionally. Freeze for 4hrs and remove butter solids. Strain through coffee filter and discard solids.

EARL GREY CAVIAR MARTINI

by Antonio Lai for Quinary, Hong Kong

Hong Kong-based Tastings Group formed in 2008 with the now-closed Tastings Wine Bar, and while that venue may now be gone, its repertoire currently includes the award-winning Quinary, as well as The Envoy, Room 309, and the Hong Kong outpost of Taipei-based Draftland by Angus Zhou.

The people behind Tastings Group are the entrepreneurial Charlene Dawes along with her right hand man Antonio Lai. Charlene also opened the now-defunct Angel's Share, since whisky was her passion. Not knowing much about the food and beverage industry then, she was consequently connected with Antonio.

Antonio Lai

It was at Quinary that Antonio became renowned for his multisensory mixology — inspired by Italian bartender Dario Comini, author of *Barchef & Molecular Mixologist* — as well as his quirky character. When the bar first opened a decade ago, Antonio implemented culinary equipment like rotary evaporators, centrifuges, sous vide machines and the like — something that hadn't really been seen or used in cocktail craft globally, let alone in Hong Kong.

The playful drinks at Quinary never cease to wow drinkers and Instagrammers alike, with unique presentations — think spicy drinks poured from mock Tabasco bottles and rainbow lollipop garnishes. But it's none other than the Earl Grey Caviar Martini and its cult status that springs to mind when one thinks of Quinary.

The drink has become so popular, the bar can sell up to a thousand a month. In fact, the volume is so high, there is one bar station solely dedicated to crafting the cocktail. Quinary also has a coin-operated machine outside the bar that's filled with merchandise, including an enamel pin in the shape of the Earl Grey Caviar Martini. I personally always take visitors to try this iconic cocktail — and always make sure to apologize to the bartenders for being cliche, but it has to be done. Long may it reign in both liquid and enamel pin form. Plus, it's always fun to see how people tackle the Earl Grey tea air.

Earl Grey Caviar Martini

One of Hong Kong's most iconic cocktails, the Earl Grey Caviar Martini has been Quinary's signature and bestselling cocktail since 2012. The cocktail engages all five senses, from its teetering tower of foam to the bursting Earl Grey caviar.

45ml	citron vodka
10ml	triple sec
20ml	apple juice
15ml	elderflower syrup
5ml	fresh lemon juice
5ml	fresh lime juice
1 slice	cucumber

Method

1. Put all ingredients and ice into a tin and shake.

2. Strain into a martini glass.

Garnish

Earl Grey tea caviar*
Earl Grey tea "air"**

*Earl Grey tea caviar

900ml Earl Grey tea; 90ml 1:1 sugar syrup^; 750ml algin water mix***

Mix all ingredients together. Add droplets of caviar mix (using a caviar box) into gluco water.**** Strain out caviar from gluco water.

**Earl Grey tea air

10g Earl Grey tea leaves; 1l hot water; 10g lecithin powder; 100ml 1:1 sugar syrup^

Brew tea leaves with hot water for 30min. Strain out tea leaves, add syrup and lecithin and mix until dissolved. Foam up with aquarium aerator.

***Algin water mix

15g sodium alginate; 750ml water

Blend until dissolved.

****Gluco Water

20g calcium lactate gluconate; 1l water

Stir until solids fully dissolved.

FLORAL
ICED TEA

by the team at Draft Land, Taipei

COCKTAILS ON TAP

Minimalist Draft Land appears to be anything but a cocktail bar upon entering. No back bar, no tools, no garnishes. The concept from Taiwanese bartender Angus Zou is more akin to a tap room than a cocktail bar — however, cocktails are exactly what's served on draft.

Draft Land was built to appeal to people intimidated by bars or worried about ordering drinks they might not like. Cocktails can be confronting, and Draft Land makes it less so by allowing guests to sample potential cocktails at the flip of a tap. The bartenders themselves are replaced by "draft tenders" instead. That's not to say the cocktails are simple: drinks here work on a draft system, and thus need to be meticulously measured, tested and consistent. Fresh fruit

Fresh fruit juices are clarified so as not to jam the lines, and egg whites are replaced with foam alternatives, since drinks are batched at up to 100 portions in one go.

Drinks are displayed on the wall where a back bar would normally sit, listed by number and their name. Should guests feel so inclined, they can look at the particular menu that tells the story of the style of drinks the tap offerings are based on. The menus have paid homage to everything from modern classics and tiki to prohibition and the golden age of drinking.

Angus says that draft tenders are serving the style, not the cocktail. He has already taken this style to several outposts in Asia, including a second branch in Taichung; a branch in Bangkok; and a branch in Hong Kong, where Angus teamed up with the city's legendary bar star Antonio Lai and the Tastings Group. Each branch serves seasonal, pre-batched and garnish-free cocktails on tap.

Floral Iced Tea

Created by Victor Chung, this is Draft Land's twist on the Beverly Hill Iced Tea. Two kinds of flower and floral baozhong tea give this strong drink a scented tea-like flavor. It's then force-carbonated to create a Champagne-like mouthfeel.

23ml	gin
23ml	baozhong rum*
23ml	osmanthus vodka**
13ml	1:1 sugar syrup^
2ml	elderflower syrup
15ml	citric acid solution***
24ml	dry sparkling wine
1 dash	saline solution^

Method
1. Shake all ingredients except sparkling win with ice and strain into an ice-filled highba glass.
2. Top up with sparkling wine.

*Baozhong rum
5g baozhong tea; 200ml white rum
Steep tea in rum for 4hrs. Strain into a bottle.

**Osmanthus vodka
5g dried osmanthus blossom; 200ml vodka
Add all ingredients to vacuum-sealed bag.
Sous vide for 4hrs at 50° C. Strain into bottle.

***Citric acid solution
6g citric acid powder: 94ml water
Stir until powder
fully dissolves into water.

FOUR WISE MONKEYS

by Max Traverse for Maka Hiki, Hong Kong

Nobody does tiki chic in Asia like Max Traverse. He mastered the art of tropical hideaways with the now-closed Honi Honi and Mahalo, and pours his years of industry knowledge and tiki talents into current venue Maka Hiki.

Tropical escapism works particularly well in densely populated concrete jungles like Hong Kong, and urban oasis Maka Hiki draws inspiration from Max's own island experiences in the Caribbean and Polynesia, as well as the tropical paradises that dot the Indian Ocean and Southeast Asia.

When the jackhammers and shoulder-to-shoulder chaos of Hong Kong become too much, one can slip inside the warm timber surrounds and verdant terrace of Maka Hiki: something of a wellness concept by day and cocktail bar by night.

Max is well versed in pineapples and punches, and Maka Hiki's comprehensive tiki menu features many a rum-based drink, including the dangerous Dum Dum Give Me Rum Rum! with four different types of rum, plus orgeat, lime juice and passion fruit puree; or the tart Maka Hiki Punch with rum, maraschino liqueur, grapefruit and lemon. Max plays with tequila tiki in drinks like the fragrant Bikini Girl with blanco tequila, lychee and rose puree, cucumber, and cranberry juice; and the spicy Tik Tok Tiki with falernum, agave syrup, lemon and grapefruit juice, blue curacao and Thai red chili.

Of course, if you're looking for the best tiki classics in town, Maka Hiki pays respects to what they call the "founding fathers of rum drinks", including a mean pina colada, daiquiris, a mai tai using famous tiki bartender Trader Vic's specifications and more.

Most drinks are served in novelty tiki cups, and huge sharing drinks come in vessels from hollowed out watermelons and pineapples or flaming volcanoes. If that's all a bit much, there are simpler rum twists on classics like a barrel-aged rum Negroni or an old fashioned.

Four Wise Monkeys

This cocktail is refreshing and spicy, but less boozy than your average tiki drink, using Indonesian Nusa Caña Spiced Rum.

50ml	Nusa Caña Spiced Rum
15ml	green apple liqueur
5ml	sugar cane syrup
35ml	fresh apple juice
10ml	lime juice
3 cubes	fresh ginger
3 dashes	tiki bitters

Method
Shake all ingredients with ice and strain into a tiki cup.

Garnish
Lime wheel with ginger sticks, flamed with aromatic bitters

FULL BLOOM

by Hidetsugu Ueno for Bar High Five, Tokyo

Bar De Luxe, Hong Kong

A Gin for All Seasons

Roku gin is made from a blend of Japanese botanicals, represented in the six-point hexagonal design of the bottle. Matching the four seasons, each botanical is harvested during its peak season: yuzu peel from winter; sakura flower and leaf from spring; sencha tea and gyokuro tea from summer; and sansho pepper from autumn. At its base, Roku also features eight traditional gin botanicals: juniper; coriander seed; angelica root and seed; cardamom; cinnamon; and bitter orange and lemon peel. Produced in Osaka, the gin is made using four different pot stills.

Nose: Notes of green tea and sakura floral give a sweet aroma.

Palate: Multi-layered with juniper as the core base flavor, and yuzu coming through as the top note. A touch of spice at the end from the sansho pepper.

Bar High Five, Tokyo

Ask anyone in the bar industry to name the first Japanese bartender that pops into their head, and I'd willingly bet a fair few Yen that they would say Ueno-san, whose career took off at Star Bar in Tokyo's Ginza district. While the man himself will admit he has become the face of Japanese bartending, he's not quite sure why, as he insists he's not a typical Japanese bartender. Perhaps his popularity is due to the fact that Ueno-san is a little non-conformist, and his approachable demeanour bridges the gap to the impeccable practice of Japanese bartending.

While Ueno-san co-owns Bar De Luxe in Hong Kong and #Findthelockerroom in Bangkok, it's his first venue Bar High Five in Tokyo that also bridges that approachability gap.

Full Bloom

Ueno-san's cocktail uses simplicity to combine Western and Japanese ingredients, highlighting the cherry blossoms that Japan is renowned for.

45ml	Roku Gin
15ml	Monin Cherry Blossom Syrup
10ml	maraschino liqueur
15ml	fresh lemon juice

Method
1. Put all ingredients and ice into tins and shake.
2. Strain into a martini glass.

While Japanese bars are incredible in their own right, they can be quiet, solemn places that may be intimidating for some. Bar High Five is welcoming, and while it still comes with its own set of rules — as is the usual custom in Japanese bars — it's frequented by drinkers from all over the world, and possesses a lively atmosphere.

That said, Ueno-san is firmly a traditionalist when it comes to making drinks. Bar High Five does not have a menu, instead whipping up classics that suit the mood of the guest. He's also a dab hand at carving almost perfect diamonds from chunks of ice — something he has become renowned for.

I've been fortunate over the years to spend time getting to know Ueno-san, and it was in doing so that I realized being idolized can be difficult for him sometimes. He's incredibly humble, but being so legendary, he admits he struggles with being doted on when visiting bars, since he prefers to see the staff take care of other guests over him — especially as he prefers not to drink.

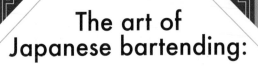

The art of
Japanese bartending:
BEYOND
TECHNIQUE

While this is predominantly a recipe book, it seems remiss to not touch on the art of Japanese bartending — arguably one of the most iconic styles of tending bar. Few countries have a distinct style, and none more so than Japan.

Modern Japanese bartenders reveal that Japanese bartending means different things to different people. For example, Shingo Gokan, founder of the SG Group, says: "It's not just about the style, it's the honoring of Japanese activities such as sado (the way of tea), judo (the gentle way) and kado (the way of flower arranging). When American bartending came to Japan, Japanese bartenders took inspiration from them, then polished their skills and techniques."

Three-piece cobbler shakers are still commonly used in Japanese bars, as these would've been the tools that the Americans brought to Japan — and they have stuck. Meanwhile, most modern bartenders prefer to use Boston shakers. Shingo says cobbler shakers are more functional, and better at circulating ice. "I also think they're used because Japanese bars are less high-volume, so they don't need to use Boston shakers for efficiency," he adds.

In addition to this, Kazuo Uyeda, author of Cocktail Techniques, founder of Tender Bar in Tokyo and creator of the hard shake, says in his book: "Westerners focus on results. While the Japanese have been influenced by this focus to a certain extent, we, at heart, respect the process."

In order to make smoother and softer cocktails, Uyeda-san developed the hard shake, in which he shakes hard diagonally in a three-point shake pattern with a snap and twist, to cause aeration that he says "prevents the bite of ingredients and sharpness of alcohol from directly attacking the tongue."

Hidetsugu Ueno, founder of Tokyo's Bar High Five, is well known for creating elaborate ice diamonds — beautifully carved ice is another defining feature of Japanese bartending. However, Ueno-san defines the style very differently. "I like to call our bartending Galapagos Islands-style, because we are all bartenders but we are a different species, developing our own style over the last century."

Ueno-san says he enjoys the focus on the small details, the way of thinking and the philosophy. "Shaking is not only back and forth and up and down. Stirring is not only rolling circles. We pour our soul into the liquid."

Ueno-san also believes the style is seeing bars as beyond just a business, with an emphasis on doing right by your guests: "We need to decline requests for more when we see a guest has had enough to drink, and have the courage to not serve them anymore. I'm sure they will be glad that they didn't have one more drink the next morning and they might come back the next day. But if we serve one more drink, they might regret it, have a hangover and probably won't come back the next day. Which is better for both of us? Bars are not a place to get drunk, bars should be a place where guests experience a joyful time."

"I call myself a psychologist without a license. We share guest's happiness, sadness and anxiousness. We laugh together, cry together and get angry together. We are here for them."

Hiroyasu Kayama, founder of Bar Benfiddich in Tokyo, says that space is important too: "Japanese bars are small, so everyone can see the beautiful movements and postures of the Japanese style, and the bartender can see the space and their guests."

Shuzo Nagumo, owner of several bars including Mixology Salon and Memento Mori in Tokyo, agrees that the bar space and ambience is important for other reasons. "Many solo guests come to Japanese bars. Some want to spend time drinking slowly, others may want to just enjoy one drink, relaxing and taking care of their mental health. Japanese bartenders always think about the hearts of all guests, hence why they tend to be quiet and value solo guests."

Shuzo also agrees Japanese bartending goes beyond just ice balls and hard shakes — it's also in how one masters a cocktail. "Japanese bartending masters the essential points of cocktails while eliminating unnecessary points. One must pursue the essence of classics and cocktails."

GARDEN CITY

by Shelley Tai for Nutmeg & Clove, Singapore

Singapore stalwart Nutmeg & Clove was founded by bartending legend Colin Chia, who is also a co-founder of Bangkok's #Findthelockerroom. The bar stays true to its locale in the Lion City with a cocktail program that tells the tales of Singapore and Asia.

To combat strict COVID-19 rules in Singapore, Nutmeg & Clove changed locations in 2021 and opened under a different type of license, which meant new decor, a new food and beverage program, and new general manager Shelley Tai. Formerly from Antonio Lai's

Colin Chia (center); Shelley Tai (right)

longstanding Quinary in Hong Kong, Shelley made a name for herself at the Diageo World Class 2019 global finals, where she ranked in the top eight representing Hong Kong and Macau.

Drinks from Nutmeg & Clove's The Cocktail Diaries menu tell the stories of Singapore through the eyes of a traveler. The menu also reveals interesting tidbits about Singapore, such as how the city state has changed time zones six times since 1905, to reflect the colony of the time — whether British or Japanese — before deciding on the current one, as told in the GMT Martini, which uses elements of Japan, Britain and Singapore in its ingredients. The menu also reveals how Singapore bans the sale of shisha and chewing gum through the Can Bubble Gum?, which is served with bubble gum "air".

K-Tea-V, a play on the abbreviation for karaoke rooms, riffs off of the classic KTV drink of whisky and green tea by pairing absinthe-infused blended malt Scotch whisky with green barley, matcha and creme de cacao. Coffee cocktail Lah Leh Meh is a nod to Singapore's coffee shop culture. Each drink tells a story through the traveler's experiences, revealing information that even locals might not be familiar with.

Garden City

Inspired by Singapore's greenery, Garden City pays homage to the Singapore Botanic Gardens, the only tropical garden in the world that is a UNESCO World Heritage site. The drink seeks to create the sights and smells of Singapore's gardens.

45ml	musk melon gin*
5ml	Empirical Spirits Ayuuk
15ml	lime juice
15ml	3:1 honey syrup^
1	shiso leaf
6	basil leaves

Method
1. Shake all ingredients with ice.
2. Strain over a large block of ice into a rocks glass.

*Musk melon gin
100g musk melon; 700ml gin
Chop melon and place into sous vide bag with gin
Sous vide at 42° C for 2hrs, then bottle.

GIMLET

by John Nugent for Kyle & Bain, Hong Kong

In the 1840s, ice was imported from America to Hong Kong's ice house storage by the Tudor Company, which shipped ice from Boston to all corners of the globe. The practice stopped in the 1850s, when ice was brought to the colony from northern China instead — that is, until the Tudor Company became the sole ice importers once again.

It wasn't until 1874 that ice was made in Hong Kong, when Scottish engineer John Kyle

patented Hong Kong's first ice machine. Kyle partnered with fellow engineer William Bain, and the pair began making ice using vapor-compression refrigeration systems at their facility, the Hong Kong Ice Works. The business's affordable prices and direct competition caused the Tudor Company to cease operations in Hong Kong and sell its equipment to Kyle and Bain. In the late 1870s, the pair sold their company to major Hong Kong conglomerate Jardine Matheson Holdings,

Gimlet

Taking inspiration from the original Gimlet recipe, Kyle & Bain's version uses a salad cordial instead of fresh lime and sugar to create a savory, full-bodied and aromatic cocktail.

30ml	genever
15ml	Nikka Coffey Gin
22ml	salad cordial*
8ml	mastiha

Method
1. Stir all ingredients into a mixing glass with ice.
2. Strain into a chilled coupe glass.

Garnish
Truffled baby peach

*Salad cordial
16g lime zest; 3g kaffir lime leaf; 3g tarragon leaves; 3
sage; 5g leeks; 6g black pepper; 300g granulated suga
510ml water; 8g malic acid; 16g citric acid
Add all ingredients except malic and citric acid into so
vide bag and seal. Let sit for 18-24hrs. Strain throug
chinois then strain through cheesecloth. Add malic ar
citric acid and dissolve.

where Bain stayed on as manager. Hong Kong Ice Works then moved to Ice House Street in Central district, before eventually closing after almost a century in business.

The pair's memory continues to live on in martini bar Kyle & Bain, located just around the corner from where the original Hong Kong Ice Works was located. The bar is John Nugent's follow-up to American-style The Diplomat, featuring a strictly stirred-not-shaken bar program, with all cocktails stirred over ice. Hidden on the mezzanine level of modern European brasserie Margo, find the secret wine bottle entrance button and be greeted by an intimate setting with colonial-inspired cocktails and various takes on martinis.

The menu is broken down to guide guests through the process of making the bar's K&B Martini — gin, dry and blanc vermouth, cider vinegar and Sicilian lemon — which is poured tableside. The key components of the martini are broken down into spirit, vermouth and ice — therefore a menu section is dedicated to spirit-forward cocktails, low-ABV drinks and those served over ice.

GIN & COCONUT

by the team at Coley, Kuala Lumpur

Chee Keong "CK" Kho (left)

Coley, in Malaysia's capital of Kuala Lumpur, takes its name from Ada "Coley" Coleman. Coleman was the first female head bartender at the American Bar in the Savoy Hotel, London from 1903 to 1925. She remained the only one until 2021. Coleman also created the cocktail Hanky Panky — one of my personal favorites — with gin, sweet vermouth, and Fernet Branca for actor Charles Hawtrey when he requested something "with a bit of punch to it."

Upon tasting the drink, he proclaimed it was "the real hanky panky", which at the time meant magic, and the name stuck. Needless to say, it's a must-have at tropical hideout Coley, along with

signatures like the addictive PB&J with peanut-infused tequila blanco, blueberry liqueur, vermouth bianco, and a pinch of salt.

Owner Chee Keong "CK" Kho has been in hospitality for over 20 years. He named the bar both as a Hanky Panky lover, as well as out of respect for the veteran bartender. CK also opened gin haven Pahit — one of Kuala Lumpur's first gin bars that went on to set a trend for gin-focused concepts — in a 1920s shophouse complete with the original floor tiling.

Pahit is named after the colonial drink of gin and aromatic bitters, known as gin pahit, often drunk by the British in British Malaya. Also known as pink gin for the pinkish hue the bitters impart, Pahit's update features London dry gin, bitters, homemade falernum syrup and lime juice.

Not being much of a gin drinker myself at the time, Coley's refreshing Gin & Coconut was a game changer for me and I knocked back my fair share on a trip to Kuala Lumpur for my 30th birthday — a trip that took me around the city's bars and got me well acquainted with one of my favorite underrated drinking scenes in Asia.

Gin & Coconut

One of the first cocktails the Coley team ever made, this straightforward drink is a taste of Southeast Asia in a glass, and remains one of Coley's best sellers.

40ml	London dry gin
150ml	young coconut water
5ml	pandan syrup*

Method
Put all ingredients into a beer mug and top it up with ice.

Garnish
Young coconut flesh and a lime twist

*Pandan syrup
500g caster sugar; 250ml water; 8 pandan leaves
On low heat, stir all ingredients together until sugar has dissolved. Let cool at room temperature and keep chilled. Keeps for up to 2wks.

HAWKER

by the team at The Bamboo Bar, Bangkok

Jazz and blues bar The Bamboo Bar in Thailand's capital of Bangkok first opened its doors in 1953. It was the city's first jazz bar, located inside the Mandarin Oriental Bangkok. While the bar was completely refurbished in 2014 and decked out with animal prints and rattan furniture, the historic venue still exudes 1950s ambience and features nightly live music performances. The likes of Louis Armstrong, Ray Charles and Dionne Warwick have performed here, just to give you an idea of its storied live music history.

The Bamboo Bar is a regular fixture on Asia's 50 Best Bars, and was the first-ever bar from Thailand to rank on The World's 50 Best Bars in 2020, when it clocked in at 35. The bar's cocktail menus often pay homage to Thailand, with the Elements menu drawing inspiration from Thailand's diverse landscapes, including city, rainforest, islands, mountains and rivers.

Cocktails from the islands section of the menu include the cheekily named Life's A Beach, with tequila blanco, curacao, dill, watermelon and almond sand, a nod to Thailand's beautiful white sand beaches and diverse array of tropical fruits. On Cloud Nine, from the mountains section, features herbs from mountainous regions, blended with bourbon, strawberry and white port.

The signatures at The Bamboo Bar also pay respects to Thailand, with the Thai Daiquiri featuring vodka, fresh lime, sugar and popular Thai ingredients pandan and lemongrass, as well as the classic Lychee Martini, thanks to Thailand's lychees being some of the best in the world.

Tequila is showcased in Hawker from the city section, and it's an ingredient that I feel is often underrepresented since it's not commonly used in classic cocktails.

I have fond memories here of parking up at the bar with my mother, who fell in love with the former head bartender Ann Pongprom. Ann got us well-oiled, and besides my mother visiting me in my previous home of Seoul and current home Hong Kong, Bangkok was the first place in Asia we visited together — and The Bamboo Bar was of course our first stop.

Hawker

Hawker is inspired by Bangkok's vast array of hawker street food restaurants. One of the team favorite dishes to have at hawker stalls after shift is tom ka gai soup: a chicken soup with coconut milk, lemongrass, galangal (ginger), kaffir lime leaf and coriander.

45ml	coconut oil fat-washed Patrón Silver Tequila*
20ml	lemongrass syrup
20ml	lime juice
2 dashes	coriander extract**
Top up	ginger beer

Method
1. Put all ingredients except the ginger beer in a shaker and shake with plenty of ice.
2. Fine strain into a highball glass full with ice
3. Top up the glass with ginger beer and give it a quick stir.

Garnish
Kaffir lime leaf

*Coconut oil fat-washed Patrón Silver Tequila
200ml virgin coconut oil;
1 bottle Patrón Silver Tequila
Mix coconut oil and Patrón Silver Tequila and sous vide for 2hrs at 60° C, or leave overnight if no sous vide. Place into wide container and put in freezer until all oil has solidified. Remove oil and strain again.

**Coriander extract
10g fresh coriander; 100ml vodka
Infuse coriander in vodka and leave for at least 2-3 hrs (overnight is best). Strain into bitters bottle.

INDO
MAI TAI

by the team at Potato Head, Bali

Potato Head beach club in Bali is a behemoth of an operation. With a capacity of 2,000, the venue can see double the number of guests during peak times. It features six bars, four restaurants and two hotels with all-day operations.

Potato Head has a strong focus on fresh produce, and the bar program is no exception. The bars mix over 600,000 drinks annually between them, and fortunately, Potato Head is arguably the epicenter of sustainable practices for the F&B trade in Asia.

Seeing the impact of environmental issues right on their doorstep due to the venue's location on the beach, the owners decided to go pedal to the metal with their efforts, working with a sustainability consultancy agency to take an in-depth look at the waste Potato Head produces and how to reduce it. Steps are taken daily to reduce energy consumption, ensuring everything in the supply chain is organic, and either recyclable or reusable.

Potato Head has shown other F&B operators that sustainable practices can actually save

Rum, the Indonesian Way

Indonesian rum (Batavia arrack) was born when the Dutch landed in Indonesia; it was made from molasses and red rice, then matured and transported back to Holland in teak wood barrels. In Holland, it was blended, bottled and sold. Throughout the 17th to 19th century, Indonesian rum was regarded as one of the bestselling and most luxurious international spirits.

Fast forward to the 21st century, where four friends with a mutual love for quality spirits and Bali (Indonesia's "Island of the Gods"), revived the forgotten story of Indonesian rum by creating Nusa Caña, meaning "island of rum".

Nusa Caña stays true to traditional Indonesian rum production, beginning with the fermentation of molasses with rice, followed by rustic pot distillation and aging in teak wood barrels. The spirit is then shipped to Holland to be uniquely blended and bottled for today's rum consumers.

Nusa Caña's core rums currently include the Tropical Island Rum and Spiced Island Rum.

Tropical Island Rum:

Nose: Green banana notes rounded by coconut and cane juice, with a hint of spice.

Palate: Fresh cane and young coconut give way to woody and toasty notes of banana leaf, finishing with vanilla.

Spiced Island Rum:

Nose: Spicy fruit cake punctuated by pineapple, with raw sugar cane and chocolatey coffee notes.

Palate: Pineapple, cacao and coffee comes through, with a long dry finish of ginger, sugarcane and nutmeg.

money, especially by eliminating single-use bar items such as plastic straws. While many think the straw conversation is now redundant, having been the initial poster child for the sustainable movement, it's worth noting how much a venue like Potato Head saves by eliminating them.

The venue uses approximately 1,450 reusable bamboo straws every day, which equals over half a million straws per year. While reusable bamboo straws cost around US$1.28, and plastic ones are US$0.14, the bamboo straw has around 12 uses, meaning a cost of US$0.10 over its lifetime, saving over US$21,000 annually.

The bars and restaurants at Potato Head have also removed single-use beverage napkins, using reusable, locally produced organic-fiber napkins and coasters in lieu. This switch saves almost US$60,000 per year and more than 10,000 plastic wraps from napkin packets.

Throughout Potato Head, most sugar has been replaced with local coconut nectar sugar or wild honey. The ingredients are transported in reusable containers from within the island of Bali; same goes for the ice. Coconuts are consumed here en masse — Bali is a tropical island after all — and are dried and shredded to be used as compost or burned to keep mosquitoes away.

This is just scratching the surface of the incredible things Potato Head does to reduce its carbon footprint, and any bar operator looking to draw inspiration on where to begin should study the beach club.

It's also a venue that holds many fond memories for me. When my first trip to Bali was coming to an end, volcanic ash caused multiple flight cancellations, so my wish to stay longer was inadvertently granted. It's also a place where I spent a lot of time at with my husband, as he was formerly the bar operations manager of Potato Head Hong Kong. He was asked over to Bali a few times to help with training, and I, being a diligent wife, of course went to keep him company... as well as make the most of this incredible venue's food, drink, pools and live music.

Indo Mai Tai

A twist on the classic mai tai, this holiday in a cocktail uses all local produce, from the Nusa Caña rum, to the fruit and pandan.

25ml	Nusa Caña Tropical White Rum
25ml	Nusa Caña Tropical Spiced Rum
20ml	housemade jackfruit and tangerine liqueur*
30ml	pineapple juice
20ml	citrus juice
10ml	pandan syrup**

Method
1. Put all ingredients and ice into a tin and shake.
2. Strain into a cup.

Garnish
Pandan leaf and fresh or dried pineapple

*Housemade jackfruit and tangerine liqueur
100g dried citrus husks including orange/tangerine (by-product from operations); 750ml vodka; 50g fresh ripe jackfruit; 100ml unrefined sugar; 100ml water
Mix all ingredients except water into jar and sous vide for 2hrs at 65° C. Let sit for 24hrs, then finely strain liquid. Add water to reduce alcohol content.

**Pandan syrup
100g pandan leaves; 500g unrefined sugar; 500ml water
Mix all ingredients into jar and sous vide for 2hrs at 80 ° C. Let sit for 24hrs and strain liquid.

JUNGLE BIRD

Asian modern classic cocktail the Jungle Bird, created in Malaysia, was — until recently — a cocktail of unknown origin. Its creation story had never been recorded, and first appeared in writing in 1989, in *The New American Bartender's Guide* by John J. Poister, where it was said to be created in 1978.

Kim Choong, founder of Malaysian bar industry publication *ThirstMag.com*, set about thoroughly researching the drink in 2020 to find the true story behind it. Choong's research led her to conclude that the Jungle Bird had been originally served as a welcome drink at the Kuala Lumpur Hilton Hotel — the city's first five-star hotel — since its opening on July 6, 1973. The name of the cocktail referred to the birds kept at the hotel that could be seen from the Hilton's Aviary Bar. The cocktail was originally served in a bird-shaped vessel, then later in a brown-green porcelain-stemmed wine goblet with a bird engraved on the side.

While the exact creation date is unknown, after many interviews and avenues, Choong discovered that the drink was created by the hotel's beverage manager, Jeffrey Ong, who passed away in early 2019 and was originally from Penang. Oddly enough, Ong was not a drinker and left the bar industry to work in the purchasing department of a hotel until he retired. I happened to be in Penang when Ong passed, and the impact he had on the Malaysian bar industry was palpable.

Tiki historian Jeff Berry listed the Jungle Bird with Jamaican rum in his 2002 book *Intoxica*, and in 2010, renowned bartender Giuseppe Gonzalez put the drink back in the spotlight by using blackstrap rum in the recipe, further swelling the Malaysian pride around one of Asia's few classic cocktails.

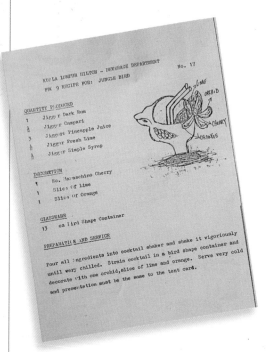

KUALA LUMPUR HILTON - BEVERAGE DEPARTMENT   No. 17
FIX 9 RECIPE FOR: JUNGLE BIRD

QUANTITY PRODUCED
1   Jigger Dark Rum
½   Jigger Campari
3   Jiggers Pineapple Juice
½   Jigger Fresh Lime
½   Jigger Simple Syrup

DECORATION
1   No. Maraschino Cherry
1   Slice Of Lime
1   Slice Of Orange

GLASSWARE
15   oz Bird Shape Container

PREPARATION AND SERVICE
Pour all ingredients into cocktail shaker and shake it vigoriously until very chilled. Strain cocktail in a bird shape container and decorate with one orchid, slice of lime and orange. Serve very cold and presentation must be the same to the tent card.

Jungle Bird

This is the original recipe listed in the 1982 Beverage Training Manual of the Kuala Lumpur Hilton.

1 jigger	dark rum
1 jigger	Campari
3 jigger	pineapple juice
½ jigger	lime juice
½ jigger	simple syrup

Method
Pour all ingredients into cocktail shaker and shake vigorously until very cold. Strain cocktail into a 13-ounce bird-shaped container and decorate with one orchid, slice of lime and orange. Serve very cold.

Garnish
1 maraschino cherry
1 slice of lime
1 slice of orange
1 orchid

KOREA COLADA

by Keith Motsi for Charles H, Seoul

Hidden in the belly of the Four Seasons Seoul, Charles H is a tribute to the life and travels of bon vivant and author Charles H. Baker Jr. His documentation of cocktails encountered during his globetrotting in *The Gentleman's Companion: Being an Exotic Drinking Book or Around the World with Jigger, Beaker and Flask* has been considered an essential read by generations of bartenders. Charles H is one of the first bars to truly celebrate the life of the imbibing icon.

The grand bar is helmed by the debonair Zimbabwe-born, UK-raised Keith Motsi, who describes Baker as "The Patron Saint of Good Living" — an accolade Keith is also deserving of, defined by his craftsmanship with a dash of mischief. Under his leadership, the bar was the first from South Korea to break into The World's 50 Best Bars in 2020.

Baker's legacy lives on through a cocktail menu inspired by his travels, which included much of Asia. Each iteration of the menu focuses on countries or cities Baker visited, featuring cocktails inspired by that place. Take the Paparazzo Cocktail in the Rome section of the menu, for example. Featuring spumante, Italian bitter blend, herbs cordial, clarified tomato and basil bocconcini, the drink is designed to transport you to Italy in just one sip. However, this is South Korea, and while featuring in the Miami section, the Korea Colada pays respects to ingredients from the bar's home turf. A take on the classic pina colada, the cocktail uses makgeolli rice wine, genever and coconut bean cream.

There are of course twists on the actual cocktails Baker encountered, such as the Far Eastern Gimlet, which he discovered in Shanghai in the 1800s. Charles H's version features its own blend of gins, lime cordial and lime blossom tea.

I lived in Seoul for a few years, way before Charles H opened, but I have had the pleasure of going back on returning visits. Along with a few other bars, Charles H has really paved the way for the cocktail boom in the city, which was largely non-existent when I left in early 2014. One thing that hasn't changed is the Korean love for drinking — so much so that Charles H has a special wheelchair service to assist inebriated guests to their room or taxi!

Korea Colada

Inspired by Baker's travels to Miami, where the pina colada is a popular cocktail, Keith's version incorporates Korean rice wine makgeolli, an alcoholic beverage that rarely features on cocktail menus.

45ml	makgeolli
20ml	genever
8ml	demerara syrup
30ml	coconut bean cream*
10ml	fresh cream
8ml	lime juice

Method
1. Place all ingredients into a tin with ice and shake vigorously.
2. Strain into a shallow cup over a large cube of ice.

Garnish
Citrus and chili oil dots, bamboo leaf, rice cake

**Coconut bean cream*
600g coconut syrup**; 15g Korean bean powder
Blend together with hand blender.

****Coconut syrup**
1kg coconut puree; 625g white sugar
Combine coconut puree and sugar and blend until it dissolves. Filter through cheesecloth. Bottle and refrigerate.

What is Makgeolli?

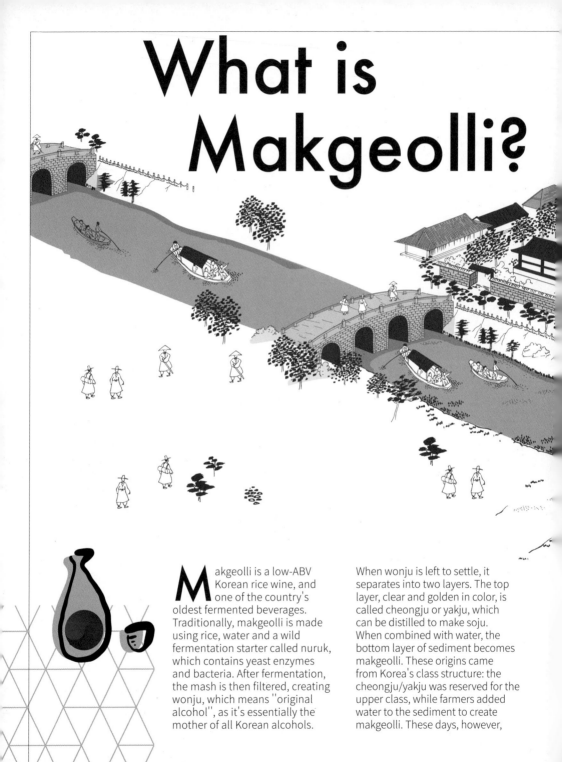

Makgeolli is a low-ABV Korean rice wine, and one of the country's oldest fermented beverages. Traditionally, makgeolli is made using rice, water and a wild fermentation starter called nuruk, which contains yeast enzymes and bacteria. After fermentation, the mash is then filtered, creating wonju, which means "original alcohol", as it's essentially the mother of all Korean alcohols.

When wonju is left to settle, it separates into two layers. The top layer, clear and golden in color, is called cheongju or yakju, which can be distilled to make soju. When combined with water, the bottom layer of sediment becomes makgeolli. These origins came from Korea's class structure: the cheongju/yakju was reserved for the upper class, while farmers added water to the sediment to create makgeolli. These days, however,

rather than removing the cheongju or yakju first, most makgeolli breweries will dilute the wonju in order to give the makgeolli the desired ABV while allowing it to retain more flavors and complexity.

Milky in color and best enjoyed unpasteurized, makgeolli comes in hundreds of variations, from mass-produced to homemade — but it is best described as slightly sweet and tangy, with a creamy mouthfeel and a slight fizz that comes from the live yeast, followed by a dry finish. Makgeolli became my

weapon of choice when I lived in Seoul, and it remains one of my favorite alcoholic beverages to drink outside of spirits. Regional variations include makgeolli flavored with nuts and fruit, with one of my favorites being the peanut makgeolli from Jeju Island.

Living in Korea, my colleagues told me that Koreans crave pajeon (savory Korean pancakes) and makgeolli on rainy days — a common ritual I was always happy to participate in.

LA PALOMA DE OAXACA

by Jay Khan for COA, Hong Kong

Hongkonger Jay Khan has been a regular fixture of the city's bar scene, but it was when he opened his own bar that his star truly ascended. His Oaxacan-style drinking den, COA — a treasure trove of agave spirits and craft cocktails — is a passion project-turned-award-winning bar, inspired by Jay's trips to Mexico. Tequila, mezcal, sotol, raicilla: you name it and COA's got it, with most bottles hand-carried by Jay and his cohorts to Hong Kong from Mexico.

While COA may not be an Asian concept, the multi-award-winning bar is arguably the epicenter for agave in the region. Jay's diligent, patient and educational approach to the agave-uninitiated has inspired legions of drinkers to shun the trauma of tequila shot-fueled hangovers, and he notes that most new mezcal and tequila drinkers aren't aware of the immense diversity in the category. Through cocktails, tasting flights and masterclasses, COA — which takes its name from the machete-like tool used to harvest agave — has achieved much since its inception, and even expanded with a second branch in Shanghai.

Aged Tequilas

So you've heard of tequila blanco, or Patrón Silver, and while this tends to be the tequila most are familiar with, there are aged tequilas called reposado (rested), añejo (aged) and extra añejo (extra aged).

Reposado is aged for a minimum of 60 days. Añejo is aged for over a year. Extra añejo tequila is aged for over three years, and therefore tends to be the most expensive variety. Each of them is rested or aged in oak, and Patrón ages in five different oak casks.

Patrón has its own reposado, añejo and extra añejo that can simply be mixed with tonic or soda, or used in place of other spirits to put an agave twist on cocktails. Silver tequila works well in gin drinks, while reposado can play the part of an aged rum, and añejo can take the place of whisky.

The bar's now famous La Paloma de Oaxaca was highly sought after, and COA collaborated with a local brewery to produce the cocktail in cans, complete with a pouch of worm salt to rim your can or glass. COA doesn't shy away from Asian ingredients, serving cocktails that combine regional specialties such as Sichuan pepper, sesame oil and shiso with Mexican chilies.

While copitas (small clay cups for drinking mezcal) and agave spirits dominate the back bar, the spirit collection here is diverse, with a solid menu of classics and even homemade horchata. Ask Jay and the team if they have any fermentation experiments on the go, and you may be lucky enough to sip some of their house tepache.

Jay's community service knows no bounds, and in late 2020, he and fellow agave enthusiast Andrew Davis created Mezcal Mission, an initiative to spread agave love for charity. This series of bi-weekly mezcal tasting experiences hosted at COA donates all proceeds to a local charity. Jay is renowned for showcasing family-owned, small-batch agave spirits known for helping their local communities, and was inspired to do the same by giving back to his community.

Much like Jay will regale how he fell in love with agave, my love affair with the category began right at his bar. I remember interviewing him a few days before COA was set to open, which turned into an impromptu tasting and education session. I was enamored with the heart and soul that goes into the making of agave spirits, which Jay conveys so well. He even inspired my very own trip to Mexico and set me on the road to becoming an agave advocate.

La Paloma De Oaxaca

Inspired by the paloma, the ubiquitous Mexican refresher of tequila and grapefruit soda, COA's adds a Oaxacan take by incorporating mezcal and an umami-laden rim of worm salt.

15ml	Patrón Silver Tequila
15ml	mezcal joven
7.5ml	fresh lime juice
105ml	grapefruit soda

Method
Build in a highball glass with ice.

Garnish
Worm salt rim and a grapefruit twist

MAESTRO MUSHROOM

by Lam Duong for Hybrid, Nha Trang

Lam Duong (center back) and team

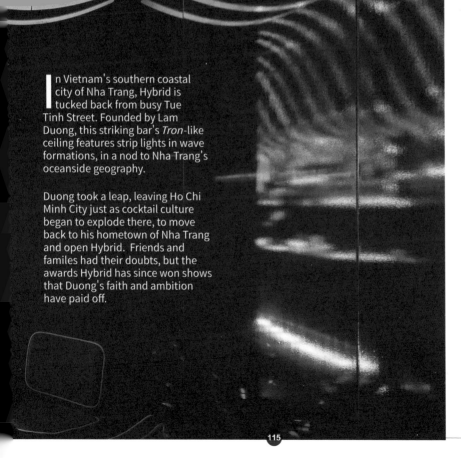

In Vietnam's southern coastal city of Nha Trang, Hybrid is tucked back from busy Tue Tinh Street. Founded by Lam Duong, this striking bar's *Tron*-like ceiling features strip lights in wave formations, in a nod to Nha Trang's oceanside geography.

Duong took a leap, leaving Ho Chi Minh City just as cocktail culture began to explode there, to move back to his hometown of Nha Trang and open Hybrid. Friends and familes had their doubts, but the awards Hybrid has since won shows that Duong's faith and ambition have paid off.

Forget what you know or want from cocktail flavor profiles here, as adventurous souls will be rewarded. The unusual flavor pairings and local ingredients that punctuate the menu feature drinks such as the Anchovy Punch, with Vietnamese white rum, coconut, fish sauce and fig leaf fat-washed with cured anchovy cream.

A less out-there creation but arguably still innovative is the Cocoa and Pink Peppercorn Negroni. Bored of mojitos? Hybrid's Black Tomato features white rum washed with chocolate milk; miso; tomato; and mint soda, and garnished with a chocolate-covered cherry tomato.

Hybrid is also a sustainability-focused bar with a zero-waste philosophy, turning any leftover cocktail ingredients into other bar products and even snacks. Think upcycled pineapple skin and mushrooms converted to pickled garnishes.

Maestro Mushroom

The Maestro Mushroom is Hybrid's take on the classic old fashioned, inspired by Lam's childhood favorite: chicken and mushroom soup.

25ml	chicken fat-washed blended Scotch whisky*
25ml	umeshu
10ml	mushroom honey lactart**

Method
1. Put all ingredients into a mixing glass.
2. Stir well with ice and strain into an old fashioned glass with an ice block.

Garnish
Pickled mushroom***

*Chicken fat-washed blended Scotch whisky
700ml blended Scotch whisky; 100ml melted chicken fat
Combine the whisky and chicken fat in jar and shake well every 2hrs for 8hrs. Put in freezer for 8hrs. Strain solids and discard.

**Mushroom honey lactart
20g shiitake mushroom; 300g raw honey; 200ml water, 8g lactic acid
Combine mushrooms and water in a vacuum bag, then sous vide for 3hrs at 75° C. Strain the liquid to get around 100-150ml of mushroom water. Mix 100ml mushroom water with honey and lactic acid until all ingredients have dissolved, then bottle.

***Pickled mushroom
20g leftover shiitake mushroom from honey mushroom lactart infusion; 200ml rice vinegar; 200g sugar; 250ml water; 5g dried chili; 5g black pepper; 1 bay leaf
Combine all ingredients except mushrooms in pan and boil on medium heat until sugar dissolves. Allow to cool and add mushrooms. Infuse for at least 1d before straining.

MARTY'S SOUFFLE

by Rusty Cerven for Manhattan, Singapore

Manhattan is arguably one of Singapore's most globally recognized bars, thanks to its domination of international awards. The bar took the number one spot on the Asia's 50 Best Bars list in 2017 and 2018, and was deemed Legend of the List in 2019. That year, Manhattan also won Best International Hotel Bar at the Spirited Awards 2019, and went on to win the inaugural Art of Hospitality Award at Asia's 50 Best Bars 2020. And that's just the top hits from their list of triumphs.

No Alcohol Required

Lyre's, the world's most awarded non-alcoholic brand, features versions of popular spirits, including Absinthe, Amaretti, American Malt, Coffee Originale, Dry London Spirit, Pink London Spirit, Aperitif Dry, Aperitif Rosso, Italian Orange, Orange Sec, Italian Spritz, Spiced Cane Spirit, White Cane Spirit, Dark Cane Spirit, Agave Blanco Spirit and Agave Reserva Spirit.

The range is made of natural flavors, extracts and distillates from fruits, botanicals, spices, seeds and other natural sources. To recreate the burn of alcohol, natural extracts such as pepper berry and other plant-based ingredients are used. The range took three years to develop, with help from one of the world's leading flavor specialists, along with highly regarded sommelier and Lyre's flavor architect, David Murphy. A catalog of more than 6,000 extracts, essences and distillates were used to create the flavors, and the entire range is vegan, nut-free and gluten-free.

No medals for guessing that the bar is a New York-inspired establishment, hailing to the golden era of cocktails and serving drinks that pay homage to the city's history, people, places and culture. The hotel bar, located in the Regent Singapore, also boasts

the world's first in-hotel rickhouse for barrel-aging spirits and cocktails. Featuring 10-foot-tall shelves stacked with 100 small barrels, signatures from the rickhouse include the aged Martinez and Solera-Aged Negroni.

The bar also has a big focus on American whiskies, with a thoroughly researched and curated list of over 220 bottles, housed in the Whiskey Glasshouse.

Manhattan has seen a wealth of well-loved and respected bartenders work there over the years, and is now led by Slovakian Rusty Cerven, a man whose resume includes the renowned Connaught Bar in London (number one on The World's 50 Best Bars 2020 and 2021 lists).

Manhattan's menus have always paid respect to New York's history, personalities, places and cultures by drawing inspiration from neighborhoods and eras. Its New York Personified menu pays homage to iconic Manhattanites such as Anthony Bourdain, Andy Warhol, Yoko Ono, Ruth Bader Ginsburg and more.

Non-alcoholic cocktail Marty's Souffle pays tribute to Ruth Bader Ginsburg and her husband Marty. Ruth's favorite place to eat was at her home in New York City, where her beloved husband Marty Ginsburg became a genuinely famous amateur chef because of Ruth's lack of skills in the kitchen. His love for cooking became so prominent that a tribute to this master chef was made in the form of a cookbook that showcased recipes that he served to his family, including Ruth's favorite dessert: frozen lime souffle.

Marty's Souffle

Marty's Souffle is a non-alcoholic take on Ruth Bader Ginsburg's favorite dessert, the frozen lime souffle, using Lyre's Dry London Spirit.

40ml	Lyre's Dry London Spirit
45ml	lime vanilla curd*
20ml	lime juice
30ml	cream
30ml	egg white
Top up	soda

Method
1. Place all ingredients except soda into a tin and dry shake.
2. Add ice into tin and shake again.
3. Strain into a rocks glass and top up with soda.

Garnish
Grated lime zest

*Lime vanilla curd
200g fine sugar; 60ml dry curacao; 4 eggs; 20ml vanilla extract; zest of 2 limes; 2 pinches of salt
Pour all ingredients into stainless steel pot and place on medium heat, stirring continuously. As soon as consistency becomes slightly thick, remove from heat and strain into bottle. Keep chilled.

MIDNIGHT BREKKIE

by Pankaj Balachandran for Bar Tesouro, Goa

B ar Tesouro is the coastal outpost of Indian industry legends Arijit Bose and Pankaj Balachandran, along with restaurateur Donovon Vaz. The pair boast impressive resumes, with Arijit making a name for himself in Singapore, moving to the city in 2014 as head bartender at 28 HongKong Street, then moving on to become a gin brand ambassador before returning to India. Arijit also co-founded The Lovers Rum with industry legend David Cordoba, former global brand ambassador for Bacardi.

Pankaj is an incredibly active member of the Indian bar community, especially through his role as a whisky ambassador, and his consultancy at Countertop, which he co-founded with Arijit. Countertop helps alcohol brands and hospitality groups build market success in India. The pair's mission is to raise hospitality standards in India and bring it to the same level as the rest of Asia.

Pankaj Balachandran (left) and Arijit Bose

"Tesouro" means treasure in Portuguese, and Bar Tesouro is tucked away in the south of Goa — an area known for its Portuguese influence. The bar's great spirit selection is unique to the city. Arijit points out that most bars are usually built to attract tourists, but Bar Tesouro is aimed at locals, providing a neighborhood bar experience with great hospitality, food, music and cocktails.

Decked out like an old Goan Portuguese house, the bar is split over two levels. One level is dedicated to dining, and the other level is the bar of course, complete with pet-friendly outdoor seating. The playful drinks menu features unique, technique-driven cocktails along with spirit-forward favorites and a few cocktails that allow local spirits to shine.

India suffered harsh lockdowns throughout the COVID-19 pandemic, and like many, Pankaj was stuck at home figuring out new hustles and ways to keep Countertop afloat via late night Zoom chats. Pankaj says one thing that was always there for him no matter what, was the peanut butter and jelly sandwich, which he spent many nights eating, washed down with cheeky shots of rum, tequila or gin.

"One thing leads to another, and my natural progression led me to think this flavor combo could become a cocktail. A friend tasted it, loved it and asked for a full bottle, and lo and behold we started selling them by the bottle for people who needed cocktails during those dark times, and it remains our bestselling cocktail," shares Pankaj.

Midnight Brekkie

This drink is inspired by Balachandran's late night snack of peanut butter and jelly sandwiches chased with shots during the dark days of lockdown.

Yield: 10 portions

500ml	Roku Gin	25g	peanut butter
100ml	bianco vermouth	7g	malic acid
200ml	watermelon juice	150ml	warm water
120ml	strawberry syrup		

Method

1. Mix malic acid and warm water thoroughly until dissolved.

2. In a blender, put strawberry syrup, peanut butter and watermelon juice and blitz until all of the peanut butter is mixed well with the liquid.

3. Add Roku Gin, bianco vermouth and malic acid. solution and leave to rest for 30 minutes in the fridge. Strain mix through coffee filter. Bottle and keep refrigerated.

To Serve

1. Pour 100ml of Midnight Brekkie into a cocktail tin.

2. Throw with ice four times.

3. Serve over a big block of ice in a rocks glass.

Garnish

Watermelon wedge

NEW DAWN

by Tom Egerton

"For sentimental reasons this probably outranks all other cocktails in our past and present life, for it was through its rosy-inspired courage we got ourselves a wife." — Charles H. Baker Jr., *The Gentleman's Companion Volume II: The Exotic Drinking Book.*

Celebrated food and drink writer Charles H. Baker Jr. traversed the world in search of good food and drinks, chronicling his travels in a tome still regarded as a must-read by bartenders. In the passage above, he is referring to the Rosy Dawn, a cocktail he sipped in Hong Kong, named for its sunrise hue. It's a drink my husband Tom Egerton and I have long been wanting to popularize, since Hong Kong doesn't have its own classic cocktail from history, like Singapore and its eponymous sling.

After many Rosy Dawns, Baker detailed his impromptu Hong Kong wedding, which began with him and fiancee Pauline Paulson drinking at a cocktail party. Fellow guest F.P. Franklin expressed her sadness that she would not be able to attend their wedding, and decided it should happen there and then. Franklin gifted the couple her own wedding ring to seal the occasion along with a small ceremony. Bottles of Krug 1923 were popped and celebrations continued into the early morning. At sunrise, Baker and Paulson departed Hong Kong Island back to Kowloon via iconic Victoria Harbour, describing the sunrise like so: "The first fingers of a rosy dawn searched up and over the stark mountains surrounding Hong Kong's superb harbor."

The original recipe is recorded as one liqueur glass each of dry gin, orange curacao and cherry brandy, plus a teaspoon of lime juice, stirred in a champagne glass over ice. Tom has recreated this exact recipe, and let me tell you: saccharine does not even begin to describe it. To be fair, the early 20th-century palate did not indulge in sugar as much as our modern diets do, so sweet drinks were more of a sought-after luxury. Baker did say that by cutting the cherry brandy and curacao to one liqueur glass, and adding a pony (or around 30ml) of cognac, the drink became drier and less sweet.

It's arguably one of the first mixed drinks recorded in Hong Kong, and Tom and I are insistent it should become Hong Kong's iconic cocktail — after an update of course, which is what Tom has done, tweaking the original ingredients and adding an Asian twist on Champagne as a nod to the Krug. I should probably point out that Tom knows his way around a bar, having grown up in and around them. He was raised in Christchurch in New Zealand, to a family that has had hospitality in their blood for generations. In fact, we met at a bar he was managing at the time. It was meant to be.

A love of the craft of cocktails has taken Tom all over the world. Most recently, he was a senior bar consultant for Proof & Company, covering a range of projects, including the award-winning ARGO at the Four Seasons Hong Kong, which also features in this book.

New Dawn

This is a modern version of the Rosy Dawn cocktail. While a great storyteller, Charles H. Baker Jr. was not a bartender, which is apparent in the original recipe. This version uses less sugary liqueurs and updates the drink with a citrus cordial in order to make it more gimlet style, and tops it with fragrant ylang ylang "sham-pagne". The ingredients pay homage to the original story, while also adding a hint of Asian tropical flavor.

40ml	London dry gin
40ml	cherry brandy
10ml	curacao
10ml	citrus cordial*
Top up	ylang ylang sham-pagne**

Method
1. Shake briskly with ice and fine strain into a Champagne flute.
2. Top up with ylang ylang sham-pagne.

*Citrus cordial
3 lemons; 2 oranges; 1 lime; 200g celery; 5g coriander seeds; 700ml 1:1 sugar syrup^
Juice all fruit and add to sous vide bag with all remaining ingredients. Seal and sous vide at 35° C for 4hrs. Strain and bottle.

**Ylang ylang sham-pagne
400ml vodka; 40g dried ylang ylang, 300ml bianco vermouth, 200ml 1:1 sugar syrup^; 2g citric acid
Combine vodka, ylang ylang and vermouth and mix with hand blender. Place blended mix in rotary evaporator flask and set to following specs until the original liquid has evaporated: temperature: 40° C; rotation: 85rpm; pressure: 20mbar; condenser temperature: -10° C. Add 150ml of distilled mix to 600ml filtered water and charge with CO_2 to carbonate

NOT YOUR MIDORI

by Jackwing Yao for Bar Sanyou, Shenzhen

The Hope & Sesame Group is South China's powerhouse married duos of Bastien Ciocca and Marcia Xiao; and Andrew Ho and Amethy Huang. The group began in Guangzhou with their first cocktail bar Hope & Sesame, followed by Italian-style cafe Charlie's, then baijiu-focused cocktail bar Bar Sanyou. They then expanded to Shenzhen with a second Hope & Sesame and Bar Sanyou, which delves further into Chinese spirits.

kwing Yao

From Austria to Hong Kong

Fernet Hunter was founded by Neville Kotewall and Raphael Holzer, and the brand has a unique and modern take on bitters. It has very much turned into an adopted Hong Kong brand, due to Raphael being based in the city, even though the product is produced in his native Austria. The blend of botanicals include arnica, orris root and lavender, which are found in the Austrian town and forest of Brunnwald and handpicked during hunting season. Fernet Hunter's other bitters, Granit, is a nod to the solid granite rocks found throughout Austria's Muhlviertel region, where many of the natural resources used to make Granit come from. Hunter differs from Granit in its dryness, increased bitter notes, and decreased sugar content, as well as the addition of aromatic chamomile.

Andrew and Bastien met while studying at the prestigious Swiss Hotel Management School, before going on to work at five-star hotels and eventually reuniting to open Hope & Sesame in 2016. Not only was the bar Guangzhou's first speakeasy, but it also used techniques rarely seen in the South China bar scene, such as centrifugal clarification and sous vide infusions.

Charlie's followed in 2019, and a year after, COVID-19 struck. The group was one of the first hit, and was recognized globally for their work during the pandemic, as they published and shared an in-depth guide to help other bar owners during lockdowns.

Three out of four of Hope & Sesame Group's bars are helmed by strong female bartenders — namely Tiger Liang, Jackwing Yao, and Lola Lau — in a scene where females behind the stick, let alone in leading roles, isn't as common. They're also known for evangelizing misunderstood Chinese spirit baijiu through Bar Sanyou, where they showcase the 12 varieties of baijiu and its versatility through cocktails.

Over the years, the group has become good friends of mine, and seeing them grow, win multiple awards and retain their humble yet knowledgeable personalities is what makes them so special. Down to earth and approachable, they're more than happy to show anyone around South China's blooming bar scene — and what better tour guides are there than those who helped kick-start it?

Not Your Midori

This drink is inspired by a more herbaceous and complex version of the Midori Sour, a cult favorite cocktail. The use of the sorghum light aroma-style baijiu adds a pear-like fragrance to the drink, which complements the cucumber and mint. By adding Fernet Hunter, it gives the cocktail a bitter element and depth, and the wasabi oil-washed rum gives the drink a pungent kick and the identity of a tiki cocktail.

30ml	Fernet Hunter
30ml	cucumber cold-brew sorghum spirit*
10ml	wasabi oil fat-washed white rum**
10ml	Midori
20ml	lemon juice
7ml	mint rock sugar syrup***

Method
1. Combine all ingredients and shake.
2. Strain over pebble ice.

Garnish
Honeydew melon wedge

*Cucumber cold-brew sorghum spirit
800g fresh cucumber; 900ml sorghum spirit
Blend ingredients for 30s before passing through conical strainer and discarding solids. Strain and bottle.

**Wasabi oil fat-washed white rum
35g wasabi oil; 300ml white rum
Mix ingredients and refrigerate at -18°C for 24hrs. Strain off oil and bottle.

***Mint rock sugar syrup
200g rock sugar; 200ml boiling water; 50g mint leaves
Dissolve rock sugar in boiling water. Allow to cool, then blend with mint leaves. Strain and bottle.

Crash Course: Baijiu Aromas

Baijiu is made from fermented sorghum, and has 12 different variations:

Light

- Usually made from wheat, barley, peas and fermented sorghum
- Floral nose and easy to drink, with a dry finish
- Mostly made in Beijing or Shanxi

Savory / Soy Sauce

- Umami and fermented bean paste-like flavor
- The most complex and expensive baijiu
- Most recognizable brand: Moutai
- Pairs well with spicier Chinese cuisines

Strong

- Fermented in ancient mud pits
- Tropical flavors followed by a long finish
- The most produced baijiu type by far

Extra Strong

- Distilled using rice, glutinous rice, wheat and corn
- A complex baijiu much like a combination of the savory, light and strong aromas
- Strong nose
- Aged for a minimum of three years

Rice

- Made from rice and rice yeasts
- Delicate honey flavors

Bean Paste / Fat

- Made from rice and aged in clay tanks with a cut of pork belly fat
- Fat imparts flavor and clarifies the liquid

Medicinal

· Made using up to 130 different types of Chinese herbs during fermentation
· Strong and fragrant nose
· Herbs impart a sweetness

Xifeng

· Named after the 3,000-year-old Xifeng distillery; its baijiu is so unique, it has its own aroma category
· Made from sorghum, barley and pea husks
· Fermented in mud pits for one year using old ropes and baskets that have been used in seafaring, imparting salt flavors
· Fresh and fruity

Sesame

· Made with sorghum, millet and barley
· Fermented in stone pits
· No actual sesame is added, but it has a nutty flavor due to its higher temperature during fermentation

Laobaigan

· Similar to vodka as made with wheat
· Stronger in alcohol than other baijiu at usually 62 to 78% ABV

Si Te

· Fermented with whole grain rice
· Mineral and citrus flavors
· Long finish

Mixed

· A blend of strong and savory types of baijiu

NOTHING

by Kenzo Lee for Twenty Fifth Hour, Hong Kong

The story behind the Nothing cocktail is a curious one. It remains unverified, but seemingly accepted — with slight variations — across the Hong Kong bartending community.

I first heard of the drink in 2019, during a bartending shift. Upon asking a guest what he'd like to order, he replied: "Nothing" — and I'm sure you can imagine the confusing back and forth that ensued. I deferred to the bar manager at the time, the talented Natalie Lau, who was notably the first and so far only Asian female to work at The American Bar at the Savoy Hotel in London. She laughed and explained the story of the Nothing cocktail to me.

According to Natalie, a local Hongkonger was drinking on his travels in the UK and asked the bartender to make him something special. Upon tasting the drink — made with vodka, melon liqueur, coconut liqueur, and fresh lemon and pineapple juice — and loving it, he asked the bartender what it was, to which he replied: "That? That's Nothing!"

Whether the bartender was palming it off as a modest nothing or there was a misunderstanding, nobody knows. Legend has it the Hongkonger brought the recipe back to the city and it became popular in nightclubs in the 1990s. Tastes changed, and the drink pretty much disappeared, save for the odd occasions when customers would bamboozle bartenders like myself by ordering it.

My husband and bar veteran Tom Egerton has a pretty solid theory. He speculates the Hongkonger in the UK may have been given a Midori Illusion — made with the infamous Kryptonite green melon liqueur Midori, vodka, triple sec, lemon and pineapple — but possibly with a twist, replacing the triple sec with coconut liqueur. He pointed out that pineapple always works with coconut, so that could be the reason it was added. Tom wonders if there was perhaps a mistranslation of illusion, meaning by the time it made the Hong Kong bartending circuit, its name became Nothing, which is essentially the definition of an illusion!

Liquor lore aside, Kenzo Lee recreated a much more palatable twist as part of Twenty Fifth Hour's cocktail tasting menu. Kenzo drew inspiration from Hong Kong's cuisine and culture to create the menu, and the Nothing is presented in two forms: half is presented in a soup bowl with roasted pineapple pieces, melon balls, parma ham and edible flowers to be consumed with a spoon, and the remaining liquid is served in a martini glass sprayed with rose water and garnished with edible flowers.

Kenzo swaps out the vodka for white rum, and to replace the coconut, he fat-washes the rum with coconut oil. Lemon juice is replaced with lime and in place of pineapple juice, he muddles pieces of roasted pineapple instead. In doing so, he creates a drink that is much more suited to 21st-century palates.

Nothing

Inspired by the Hong Kong classic Nothing, Kenzo updates a sweet drink reflective of the 1990s palate and brings it up to date with quality ingredients and an innovative serve.

20ml	coconut oil fat-washed white rum
40ml	melon liqueur
15ml	fresh lime juice
10ml	1:1 sugar syrup^
3 pieces	roasted pineapple

Method
1. Pan-fry fresh pineapple pieces until caramelized.
2. Muddle roasted pineapple in a shaker.
3. Add all other ingredients into the shaker and fill with ice.
4. Shake, strain and pour half into a martini glass and half in a soup bowl.

Garnish
Roasted pineapple pieces, melon balls and parma ham

*Coconut oil fat-washed white rum
300ml coconut oil; 750ml white rum
In container, add oil and rum. Leave to sit in cool, dark place for 5hrs. Shake every hour or so to agitate. Place container in freezer and leave overnight, or up to 8hrs. Remove from freezer and carefully strain out alcohol using coffee filter and funnel into your chosen bottle.

NSC
GIN & TONIC

by Juan Yi Jun for No Sleep Club, Singapore

Juan Yi Jun and Jessica "Hutch" Hutchinson are the dream team behind Singapore's rebellious No Sleep Club. The bar started life as a tiny hole in the wall, doing takeaway coffee by day and cocktails by night. Since moving to a larger venue on popping Keong Saik Road, the all-day concept focuses equally on wine, cocktails, food and coffee.

While Singapore's bar scene is world class, there are many glitzy, upmarket cocktail bars — and No Sleep Club sticks its middle finger up at this idea by creating a casual, welcoming space with edgy punk branding and an atmosphere that allows you to easily hunker down for hours on end.

Jun admits the concept was born out of wanting to create the kind of bar she and Hutch would want to work at, after finding there was nothing of the sort. "We had toyed with the idea of working abroad, but that was only because we couldn't find anything in Singapore that we felt suited us. So instead of packing our bags, the conversations led to making a category just for us." Luckily, it seems that what Hutch and Jun

Jun and Hutch

love is also what is popular with the people, as the bar has since skyrocketed to acclaim, and made its debut on The World's 50 Best Bars 2021 list at number 26.

Hutch and Jun are both wine nuts, and their list of weird and wonderful natural wines features bottles rarely seen in Asia, but it's hard to choose when the cocktail list is also a banger in its own right. Quirky flavor combos like Hay and Apples (fresh toasted hay whisky; chamomile honey; fresh and fermented apples) or the Tom Yum and Melon (Thai herb distillate; blue ginger gomme; carbonated melon) make a welcome alternative to plain ol' highballs.

Over the years, the pair have become my good friends. Hutch especially, with her unicorn magic and energy, brightens any room, and on the rare occasions we get to hang, it's always full of fun and laughing-until-our-faces-hurt. I'm really proud of the pair for creating the bar I wish I'd have dreamt up!

NSC Gin & Tonic

This is No Sleep Club's take on the gin & tonic, based on the simple combination of fresh guava and sour plum sugar which Jun grew up with, as her mum would put them out after dinner for a simple but delicious dessert.

30ml	plum gin*
10ml	guava syrup**
7.5ml	sakura vermouth
15ml	lime juice
50ml	tonic
30ml	soda
2 pinches	dried sour plum powder

Method
1. Rim half a highball glass with dried sour plum powder.
2. Combine the rest of the ingredients into a tall highball glass full of ice.
3. Zest with lemon and discard.

Garnish
Slice of fresh guava

*Plum gin
6 red or yellow plums to 1 bottle of gin
Slice plums and add to gin in a covered container. Leave to rest at room temperature, or somewhere warm, for 24hrs or until it turns dark pink.

*Guava syrup
Equal parts guava juice and caster sugar; sea salt
Juice guava. Measure and add equal weight in sugar. Add to pot and bring to boil. Remove from heat when sugar dissolves and cool. Add 1g of sea salt for every 500ml.

NYONYA BUSINESS

by Joshua Ivanovic for JungleBird, Kuala Lumpur

A bar continuing to keep Malaysia's iconic drink, the Jungle Bird, alive is the eponymous JungleBird in Kuala Lumpur's Bukit Damansara. Opened by couple Lolita Goh and Joshua Ivanovic and their business partner Divyesh Chauhan, the bar is a nest to all things rum, or as they call it, the "Rumah Rum", meaning "house of rum" in local language Bahasa Melayu.

In a city accustomed to whisky and gin, the trio have paved the way for cane spirits, with over 300 different bottles on offer. They've turned many a naysayer into a rum convert, all while educating their guests on the diversity of what is one of the fastest growing spirit categories.

Divyesh Chauhan, Lolita Goh, Joshua Ivanovic

While many would be quick to categorize JungleBird as a tiki bar, the team prefers to call their design concept "Malaysiana", featuring rattan, natural materials and lush greenery. The bar moved locations in 2020, with the team building most of it by hand using construction skills learned from online tutorials.

The cocktail menu features a number of creations designed to reflect the cultures of the world's rum-producing nations, such as Put The Lime In Ti' Coconut, which uses rhum agricole from Martinique, coconut, mint and citrus. Staying true to its roots, JungleBird also has a section of cocktails influenced by Malaysia, such as the Chendol Colada, inspired by the popular iced sweet dessert and paired with rum, JungleBird coconut cream, pandan and pineapple.

Nyonya Business

Inspired by typical Peranakan flavors, Nyonya Business celebrates the town of Melaka on the west coast of peninsula Malaysia, which is famous for the production of fermented shrimp or cincalok. Cincalok is a key ingredient used in the production of rojak, a sweet sauce made from fermented shrimp, sugar, lime, chili and sesame.

40ml	white rum
20ml	fresh pineapple juice
30ml	cucumber and green chili shrub*
20ml	cashew orgeat**
12ml	rojak syrup***

Method
1. Shake all ingredients and serve short over cubed or block ice in a cup.

Garnish
Cucumber ribbon

*Cucumber and green chili shrub
500ml cold pressed cucumber juice; 60ml apple cider vinegar; 80ml rice vinegar; 250g sugar; 12 green bird's eye chili; 2bsp salt
Stir vinegars, salt and sugar into cucumber juice until dissolved. Chop chili, add to mix and allow to infuse for 12hrs chilled, shaking occasionally. Strain out chili and bottle.

**Cashew orgeat
300g cashew nuts; 300ml water; 300ml unsweetened almond milk; 1bsp salt; sugar
Roast cashews in pan on low heat until slightly black on one side. Blend with water, almond milk and salt. Strain, weigh and cut 1:1 with sugar.

***Rojak syrup
10g white sesame seeds, lightly toasted and ground; 100g groundnuts toasted and ground; 2 tbsp palm sugar; 2 tbsp sweet soy sauce; 2 tbsp black shrimp paste; 1 tsp dried fermented shrimp paste, toasted and ground; 2 tbsp tamarind juice (combine 1:1 tamarind pulp and warm water and strain); chili paste/powder; fine sea salt
Add all ingredients except for chili and salt to mixing bowl and stir to combine until it becomes thick paste. Add chili and salt to taste. Combine 1:1 rojak sauce and water and stir well to dissolve.

OLD FASHIONED

by the team at Jigger & Pony, Singapore

Indra Kantono and Gan Guoyi were two young twenty-somethings when they met in a beer bar in Singapore. Numbers were exchanged, they began dating, and the rest is history — although I am more inclined to say the rest is legacy, as the two have since created the F&B empire that is the Jigger & Pony Group, with seven venues and bottled cocktail brand PONY in their stable (pun intended).

Guoyi was a flight attendant, Indra was working in banking, and one day they found themselves shooting the breeze with friends, when one asked: If you could do anything you want, what would you do? Indra's dream was to open boutique hotels in Bali, and Guoyi's was to open a bar. Realizing a bar might not be too far-fetched, the pair set about researching.

Indra trawled magazines and the web, kickstarting the pair's obsession with classic cocktails — which were not really available in Singapore at the time. Guoyi would do the "field research", bargain-hunting in liquor shops abroad to source products not available

at home. The couple would host weekly gatherings at their home, creating a cocktail menu using their home bar stocked with Guoyi's finds, serving snacks and getting feedback on the drinks from friends.

Things started to get serious and Guoyi resigned from her job to focus on finding a location, but it wasn't easy. Before securing the location, the pair were constantly outbid and faced many hurdles.

On Chinese New Year in 2012, Indra and Guoyi had some time to kill and decided to visit a temple, even though they are not religious. They were met with a long queue, as most people want to be the first to enter the temple at the stroke of midnight, placing their joss sticks and praying for the new year. Just before midnight, ashes from joss sticks began to fill the air, and it started to rain, all on the eve of the year of the Water Dragon.

By some miracle, Guoyi was one of the first to place her joss sticks at the temple. Three weeks later, they finally got a lease, securing Jigger & Pony's first location on Amoy Street. "We are superstitious business people now," laughs Indra. He also jokes that the bar was the most expensive engagement ring ever.

Guoyi operated the bar, with Indra working fulltime in banking, pulling shifts on evenings and weekends, and eventually quitting his banking job. In 2014, they opened Sugarhall next to Jigger & Pony, and this set the ball rolling for even more venues as the Jigger & Pony Group expanded.

The year 2018 was a particularly pivotal and challenging one for the group. The couple had signed a lease for a big and expensive project: bar and restaurant Caffe Fernet. It's worth noting that Jigger & Pony Group has never had investors, in order to maintain full ownership. So when the landlord of Sugarhall and Jigger & Pony — which had recently been renovated — gave them six months notice to leave the building due to redevelopment, things were particularly devastating.

Indra says there was no margin of safety with Caffe Fernet, so they immediately made the decision to reopen Jigger & Pony, securing the current location — at double the size — at the Amara Hotel in late 2018. Sugarhall took a longer hiatus, reopening in 2022.

The team was hesitant at the thought of Jigger & Pony being a hotel bar, but Indra says they used the opportunity to turn Jigger & Pony into the living room of the city. "Hotel bars can often be a safe cocoon for travelers in unfamiliar environments. But when I travel, I want to be immersed in the city's culture and go to places that embody that spirit. We reflect what Singapore's about: diversity, a love for cocktails, high energy and top service," says Indra. Two years later in 2020, Jigger & Pony was awarded the top spot at Asia's 50 Best Bars, proving the couple's gamble at a hotel bar had paid off.

Indra says that while they don't claim to be bartenders — their partner and bar director Aki Eguchi takes care of this — they just have an undying love for hospitality. The group's DNA is convivial hospitality. "Our brand is friendly, welcoming and without judgment," says Guoyi. "Our focus is on growing cocktail culture and turning guests to cocktails they may not have encountered before."

Old Fashioned

The bar's most iconic drink has been refined over the years. It's the king of classic cocktails, and Jigger & Pony is the champion of them. Indra says the drink is garnished with three citruses and a cherry, marrying American and Japanese cocktail styles.

45ml	Maker's Mark Bourbon
5ml	1:1 demerara syrup^
3 dashes	aromatic bitters

Method
1. Combine ingredients over a block of clear ice in a mixing glass and stir.
2. Strain into a rocks glass over a large ice cube.

Garnish
Citrus wheel with amarena cherry on a garnish pick

PEGU CLUB

by Jen Queen for Pegu Club, Yangon (archives)

In Yangon, Myanmar, a 24,000-square meter property lies decaying, having witnessed years of war and coups. Originally constructed from teak in the 1800s, the Pegu Club served British officers and colonial officials stationed in Rangoon, Burma — as the city and country were known at the time. A gentlemen's club full of British royalty and writers like Rudyard Kipling and George Orwell were known to post up at the club over the course of its history. It was also the first place in the country to have ice, making it a popular spot for cocktails.

The original Pegu Club is said to have burned down during a Japanese bombing raid in 1941 and was rebuilt after World War II, operating for a short while post-Burmese independence and eventually closing in 1965. A Burmese family later obtained a long term lease on the Pegu Club, aiming to restore the property. It was partially open for a brief period before the COVID-19 pandemic and subsequent military coup put a stop to its activities, but the eponymous cocktail lives on.

Someone who is well versed in the history of the club and the cocktail is former Yangon-based bartender Jen Queen. Jen was brought on in late 2020 to consult on the bar operations of Pegu Club on opening night. She now manages The Pontiac in Hong Kong, after unfortunately having to flee when the military coup began in 2021.

Even after extensive research, Jen couldn't unearth who created the original drink. While it was likely the signature at the club, Jen discovered the earliest recording of the drink was in Harry MacElhones's ABC of Mixing Cocktails in 1921. The recipe is listed as: 1 dash of Angostura bitters, 1 dash of orange bitters, 1 teaspoonful of lime juice (Rose's), ⅙ curacao (orange), ⅔ gin. It's highly unlikely that cordial was used in Myanmar, due to the abundance of fresh fruit.

Throughout her bar career in Yangon, Jen made it a point to educate drinkers on the Pegu Club and teach Burmese bartenders how to make it. "The reason we'll never really know who made the drink is probably due to the colonial mindset of the time — I doubt anyone wanted to give credit to a Burmese bartender. I told the people I served it to, or trained, to decolonize it, and make it theirs, especially as there are very few classic cocktails originating from Asia."

Pegu Club originally had a sign that stated "No women. No Burmese. No dogs" — and Jen says that being able to update the recipe and tend bar at the club as a woman was a huge honor.

Jen's tweaking of the cocktail was difficult due to the availability of liquors in Myanmar, and she notes that the original gin at the base of the cocktail was likely a Rangpur gin from India, given that it was a nearby British colony. Some argue that orange bitters shouldn't be included in the recipe, but Jen thinks it should be, and keeps it in her version. Curacao is difficult to get a hold of in Myanmar, and while Jen says both Cointreau or curacao work, Cointreau gives the drink more vegetal notes and pushes forward different accents from the bitters.

Pegu Club

This is an updated take on the original Pegu Club, using Cointreau in place of curacao. For those who prefer a drier drink, omit the sugar syrup.

60ml	The Botanist gin
10ml	Cointreau
15ml	fresh lime
1 dash	aromatic bitters
1 dash	orange bitters
5ml	1:1 sugar syrup^

Method

1. Combine all ingredients in tins and shake.
2. Strain into a chilled coupe glass.

PISTACHIO SOUR

by Sandeep Kumar for The Wise King, Hong Kong

The Wise King, founded by Hong Kong bar veteran Sandeep Kumar, takes its name from King Alfonso X of Castile, who was known as The Wise King. King Alfonso X's reign during the 13th century was known as a decadent one, with the monarch ordering that taverns could not serve wine to customers unless it was accompanied by a small snack. Because of this, he is credited with inadvertently inventing tapas.

The bar is tucked away behind a mural of The Wise King himself, leading into a small, windowless venue decked in red and gold, creating a "What happens at The Wise King stays in The Wise King" feeling of regal luxury and debauchery. The decor is inspired by Old World dressing lounges, with damask wallpaper, as well as antique dressers and cabinets dotting the space. The bar was one of the first in the city to inspire a spate of independent, bartender-owned venues following on from the success of neighboring COA and The Old Man.

The menu features simple yet punchy flavor combinations. While classic in style, the bar still incorporates culinary techniques such as reductions and sous vide cooking in its cocktails. And of course there's a small menu of tapas such as Spanish cheeses and cold cuts, croquetas and patatas bravas.

The Wise King's take on classics includes the Jamon Old Fashioned, infusing one of Spain's favorite tapas in bourbon, then blending it with cantaloupe syrup and walnut bitters. Meanwhile, the Pickled Margarita features bay leaf-infused reposado tequila, mezcal, pickled beetroot shrub, citrus and cayenne. The bar program also features claypot-aged cocktails such as Olla De Barro Dos, with bianco vermouth, americano bianco and eight-year-old brandy with brined gherkin.

The team are also fans of Spanish favorites sherry and gin, which they will happily recommend with a tonic, and the menu nods to Italy with the signature King's Negroni and Pistachio Sour.

Pistachio Sour

The Pistachio Sour is inspired by the classic Sicilian dessert, the torta pistachio e ricotta.

40ml	white rum
30ml	buttered pistachio shrub*
7.5ml	lemon juice
7.5ml	lime juice
20ml	homemade ricotta foam**

Method
1. Shake all ingredients except foam with ice and strain into a Nick & Nora glass.
2. Top with homemade ricotta foam.

Garnish
Finely grated pistachio

*Buttered pistachio shrub
1kg pistachios; 1kg sugar; 1l water
Add all ingredients to sous vide bag, seal bag and cook for 2hrs at 65° C, then blend. Place in conical strainer and press to squeeze milk from pistachios. Chill for 12hrs, shaking occasionally. Strain and bottle.

**Homemade ricotta foam
800ml milk; 200ml cream;
5ml lemon juice; 1g citric acid
Mix all ingredients with hand blender before placing in iSi cylindrical stainless steal canister and charging with cream charger before use.

POKER GAME

by Andy Loudon for Tippling Club, Singapore

Singapore's Tippling Club is a bar and restaurant by chef-owner Ryan Clift, with head bartender Andy Loudon behind the stick. The space is renowned for both its food and drink, with ex-head bartender Joe Schofield leading the bar to acclaim with his fairly-bonkers-yet-genius menus.

Tippling Club's previous Sensorium menu was a collaboration with American fragrance specialist International Flavors & Fragrances (IFF), where the menu was presented in fragrance strips. IFF created 12 fragrances based around emotive words such as rain, leather, grass and campfire. Joe and Ryan then designed 12 cocktails based on the fragrances IFF created, with the Rain cocktail boasting earthy aromas, or petrichor — that indescribable smell after rain. Without any further description, guests had to choose their cocktail based solely on the aroma and the single word.

Andy Loudon

Joe's follow-up was the Dreams & Desires menu, in which guests were handed a candy shop bag with 12 different gummy bears representing dreams and desires such as happiness, peace and supercar. They had flavor profiles such as white wine, butter, citrus, gin and petrol. Guests were encouraged to sample the gummy bears before committing to the cocktail.

Andy had big shoes to fill after Joe, but he has managed to design menus equally as sense-provoking in his volumes, entitled A Guide to Modern Drinking. The menus are inspired by modern art and celebrated artists.

Cocktail Poker Game is a nod to the famous painting *Dogs Playing Poker* by Cassius Coolidge. Andy designed the drink to represent all the flavors and aromas that one would associate with a game of poker, explaining: "Whenever I play poker, I always smoke a cigar and drink American whiskey. Cedar wood is generally the wood used in making a cigar box of good quality, hence its use in the incense we smoke the glass with, before serving along with frankincense and marshmallow root."

"We then make a blend of bourbon and rye whiskey and add the Hyogo smoked vinegar for structure rather than acidity," Andy continues. "Hyogo smoked vinegar comes from Japan's Hyogo prefecture, and is made using smoked cherry wood chips. The inclusion of hay syrup came from me envisioning playing a game of poker in the Wild West — with tumbleweeds blowing past."

Poker Game

Poker Game is inspired by the aromas and flavors associated with a game of poker, as well as the painting *Dogs Playing Poker* by Cassius Coolidge.

25ml	high proof bourbon
25ml	rye whiskey
10ml	organic hay syrup*
1.25ml	Hyogo smoked vinegar
5 dashes	tonka bean bitters**

Method
Stir over ice and strain into a rocks glass.

Garnish
Edible playing card

*Hay syrup (yield: 200ml)
30g dry hay; 1l 1:1 sugar syrup^
Add all ingredients to sous vide bag and seal. Sous vide for 1hr at 56° C. Strain liquid, discard hay and store syrup.

**Tonka bean bitters
1 tonka bean; 100ml Peychaud's bitters
Grate tonka bean and add with bitters into sous vide bag and seal. Cook for 30min at 56° C. Strain liquid and put into bitters bottle.

POMELO

by Ronnaporn Kanivichaporn for Mahaniyom, Bangkok

I'll never forget the moment I first met Ronnaporn "Neung" Kanivichaporn. My husband Tom had already met him previously, and we'd arranged to meet at his bar, Backstage, on a visit to Bangkok. We walked in, and like a James Bond villain, Neung swiveled round on a red velvet chair and purred, "Hellooooo Tom." He was wearing his signature black T-shirt with white text stating: "RonnaPORN wanna be a STAR", with the words porn and star aligned appropriately (or inappropriately, depending on whom you ask). I was sold.

Neung is a real character — it's hard not to be when you're an ex-model, singer and TV presenter — and his journey into bartending is a little more unconventional. As a youngster, he always enjoyed the sweet and luminous cocktails he encountered at bars and clubs, which inspired him to buy cocktail books and learn more. He later got a job at a nightclub, which allowed him to play around with drinks and experiment.

In 2011, the Diageo World Class competition came to Thailand, and Neung was asked to emcee the competition for the next few years. "Every time I saw the competitors making drinks, I fell more in love with cocktails. I felt as if I'd found a community that spoke the same language," says Neung.

In the 2012 competition, as the emcee, Neung joined all the classes Diageo provided and always created his own drinks based on the challenges given to competitors, listening and learning from the judge's feedback.

In 2014, Neung actually joined the competition, and when he visited Singapore to compete in the Southeast Asia final, things accelerated. "Seeing proper bars in Singapore blew my mind. We didn't really have anything like that in Thailand at the time," he says. He went on to win the regional final, representing Thailand in the global finals in the UK.

Neung opened Backstage with his partners in 2016, and #Findthephotobooth in 2018, but both unfortunately fell victim to the COVID-19 pandemic. #Findthelockerroom, which opened in 2017, is still going strong. Neung opened the bar with his longstanding business partner Janz Bhumichitr and fellow bartending legends Colin Chia (Nutmeg & Clove Singapore), Hidetsugo Ueno (Bar High Five, Tokyo) and Nick Wu (Bar Mood, Taipei).

In 2019, Neung entered the Bacardi Legacy cocktail competition, and won the global final with his drink Pink Me Up made with white rum, fresh tomato, orgeat, lemon juice, olive brine and fresh basil. He'll be the first to admit why he entered so many competitions, saying: "I love free trips! Who doesn't?"

Neung has now opened bar Mahaniyom (meaning "popular" in Thai) with Janz, above acclaimed restaurant 100 Mahaseth. With modern Thai decor and an energetic vibe that doesn't take itself too seriously, the bar is much like Neung. Drinks here take one ingredient, such as pineapple, and use every part from peel to juice, pulp, leaf and more. Think orange skins to make vermouths, pulp for hydrosols and pith to create bitters.

"The extraction of flavors via the understanding of local ingredients through their life span, derivatives and various forms, are the building blocks to our resourceful cocktails," explains Neung.

Pomelo

This cocktail showcases every part of the pomelo fruit in several forms.

45ml	white rum infused with rice paddy herb*
10ml	bianco vermouth
30ml	pomelo saccharum cordial**
30ml	pomelo juice
45ml	pomelo leaf tea***
2 drops	chili tincture****

Method
1. Throw the drink between tins with ice.
2. Strain into a stemless wine glass with ice.

Garnish
Pomelo pulp cracker*****

*White rum infused with rice paddy herb
100ml white rum: 5g fresh rice paddy herb
Put all ingredients into sous vide bag and sous vide at 55° C for 30min.

**Pomelo saccharum cordial
300g pomelo peel; 300g sugar; 50ml water
Cover pomelo peel with sugar and leave for 72hrs at room temperature. Add water, mix and strain, discarding solids.

***Pomelo leaf tea
Dehydrate pomelo leaves, then blend into tea powder. Brew with hot water (2g tea to 100ml water).

****Chili tincture
10g dried chili; 100ml vodka; 10ml Peychaud's bitters; 100g pomelo pith
Infuse all ingredients together for 24hrs.

ROMA GIMLET

by Lorenzo Antinori for ARGO, Hong Kong

While many major Asian cities boasted grand, crowning-jewel hotel bars, Hong Kong was fairly lacking — until ARGO opened in 2021. Housed in the Four Seasons Hong Kong, ARGO is helmed by Lorenzo Antinori, a man whose resume includes London's The Savoy and Dandelyan, as well as Charles H in Seoul; and Summer Lo, Four Seasons stalwart and winner of Asia's 2019 edition of all-female speed bartending competition Speed Rack.

ARGO is named after the ship in the ancient Greek myth in which Jason and the Argonauts sailed to claim the Golden Fleece, but the bar's mission is far from ancient. Forecasting the future of drinking, ARGO's menu highlights ingredients once classed as luxuries — such as vanilla, cacao and coffee — which may once again become luxuries due to climate change. Cocktails are presented two ways: one is inspired by the origin of the ingredient, and the other is forecasting how this ingredient may change in the future.

A Distinctly Chinese Gin

Peddlers, a premium Shanghai brand, distills rare Eastern botanicals to create a gin inspired by various regions of China. Named for Shanghai's history as a merchants' hub and for the traditional street culture that still exists today, Peddlers features botanicals from China like Gansu lotus, Buddha's hand, Sichuan peppercorn and Tianshan almonds. Double distilled in a copper still in batches of 250 bottles, the first stage sees the liquid and a majority of the botanicals put in the still to macerate for 24 hours before distillation. On the second distillation, East Asian mint and Buddha's hand are vapor-infused, to capture the fragrances of these delicate ingredients. The product is all made on site, from distillation to bottling and labeling.

Nose: Earthy, with top notes of mint, citrus and distinctive Sichuan pepper.

Palate: Strong juniper followed by angelica, cinnamon and licorice with aromatic citrus and honey notes. Finishes with numbing spice from the Sichuan pepper.

ARGO's spirits menu, dubbed the Field Guide, showcases some of the world's most innovative spirits, categorized into five sections: Modernist Spirits; Collaborative Creations; Philanthropic and Socially Conscious; A Sense of the Land; and Clash of the Worlds. Take Monker's Garkel Gin, under Modernist Spirits: Monker's Garkel is the world's first gin created entirely by artificial intelligence, using a "Gin Neural Network" that analyzed thousands of gin recipes before deciding the final botanicals, the name and the label design.

ARGO's Martini, with its own bespoke gin and served with a citrus or savory hydrosol, has fast become iconic, along with its quirky welcome drink: a small coupe of champagne with a gummy bear at the bottom. The bar also collaborates with several Asian producers to source ingredients, such as cacao from Malaysia and local Hong Kong honey.

ARGO is very close to my heart — my husband, bar professional Tom Egerton, consulted on the project. I saw the idea morph, develop and bloom over the years and while of course I'll always wax lyrical about the bar, I'm genuinely bowled over with pride at the final product. Another cherry on top is Summer being part of the team, as well as the Speed Rack Asia 2019 winner. I was the organizer of this competition after convincing the founders — who started in the US — to let me bring it to Hong Kong. Her winning against the competition from all over Asia and being our hometown hero was another proud moment.

Roma Gimlet

The ARGO gimlet evolves seasonally, and the team simply swaps certain ingredients with others, without changing the ratios. The key seasonal ingredient is introduced via the main spirit base, allowing the team to keep a very approachable DNA. In this case, the sweet local tomatoes pair fantastically with the savory Sichuan pepper notes in Peddlers Gin.

40ml	Roma tomato Peddlers Gin*
10ml	horseradish vodka
15ml	1:1 sugar syrup^
15ml	acid solution**
2 dashes	apple cider vinegar

Method
Stir all ingredients and strain into a coupette.

Garnish
Tomato olive oil drops***

*Roma tomato Peddlers Gin
700ml Peddlers Gin; 200g fresh Roma tomatoes
500g white sugar; 500g apple cider vinegar
Chop tomatoes, combine with other ingredients and blend everything together. Strain through coffee filter. Bottle and refrigerate.

**Acid solution
35g malic acid; 25g citric acid; 1l water
Combine all ingredients until acid dissolves.

***Tomato olive oil drops
1 part passata; 1 part olive oil
Blend together and strain through coffee filter. Transfer into pipette.

SIKHYE

by Demie Kim for Zest, Seoul

Zest, opened by Korean bar veterans Demie Kim, Sean Woo, Jisu Park and Noah Kwon, focuses on Korean design, food and drinks. With minimal waste in mind, the bar uses locally grown products from producers to build what Zest calls a "sustainable fine drinking culture where environment, community and people exist together in harmony."

The decor is Korean minimalism, with no bottles displayed in the back bar and no garnishes without a purpose. The bar features a prep lab that guests are welcome to visit to see how Zest's drinks are prepared.

The menu aims to make the most of whole ingredients. Take for example the Jeju Garibaldi, which uses the juice of Jeju oranges, from Jeju island in the south. The peels are then redistilled into Zest's house gin and leftover pulp from juicing is collected and either turned into cordial or fermented to make an in-house pulp sauerkraut. Zest also has a house soda system where the team makes their own soda, tonic, and even cola using upcycled ingredients, meaning no soda PETs or aluminum can waste is generated by the bar.

Sikhye is a Korean rice beverage dessert made with cooked rice, malted barley and spices such as ginger and cinnamon. There are many variations of sikhye, but the team's favorite is the sweet pumpkin variety. Zest's cocktail of the same name is mixed with Tokki Black Organic Rice Soju; their house rum blend of Plantation Original Dark Rum; and Plantation OFTD Rum infused with various spices. It is then clarified with milk, making it Zest's take on a milk punch. Demie says the result is a toasty, tropical and silky cocktail that is truly Korea in a glass.

Sikhye

Sikhye is a clarified milk punch take on the popular Korean rice beverage of the same name.

Yield: around 40 portions

500ml	Tokki Black Organic Rice Soju
250ml	Plantation Original Dark Rum
150ml	Plantation OFTD Rum
750ml	pumpkin sikye
750ml	spice mix*
450ml	milk
75ml	warm water
75ml	lemon juice
5g	agar agar

Method

1. Add all 3 acids to warm water and dissolve. Set aside 75ml.

2. Warm sikhye and the milk separately to 60° C. In a large container, add milk, Plantation Original Dark Rum and Plantation OFTD Rum mixture, sikhye and spice mix.

3. Strain carefully while pouring. Add lemon juice to curdle solution.

4. Rest in the fridge for at least 2 hours. Strain with a cheesecloth, bottle and refrigerate.

To Serve

1. Pour 60ml of Sikhye batch into a rocks glass over a large ice cube and stir.

*Spice mix

750ml water; 7.5g cinnamon; 7.5g cassia bark; 7.5g dried jujube; 5g curcuma; 4g Korean pepper; 4g clove; 4g star anise; 4g cardamom pods; 2.5g salt; 450g white sugar

Add all ingredients except sugar in pot, and bring to boil. Reduce to a low heat , add sugar and steep for 15min. Add agar agar and whisk.

SINGAPORE SLING

by Ngiam Tong Boon and Proof & Company for Long Bar, Singapore

The Singapore Sling, created by Hainanese bartender Ngiam Tong Boon, is undoubtedly Asia's most recognized cocktail, and originates from Long Bar at the Raffles Hotel. Hotel legend has it that this creation of Boon's in 1915 enabled women to consume alcohol secretly, as during the early 1900s, women could not drink alcohol in public. Boon created this boozy cocktail masquerading as a pink fruit juice to make it appear innocent to men that were none the wiser, therefore making it socially acceptable. I like to imagine Boon winked knowingly at every woman getting sozzled from this secret concoction.

This story as told by Raffles, while endearing and nostalgic, may have been embellished for the sake of romanticism, and unfortunately the original recipe has been lost. However, looking back through history, the Singapore Sling's origins may not have started as the pink drink we know today.

Older than the cocktail itself, slings — which were traditionally made of spirit, water and sugar — were popular in 18th and 19th-century America. One of the earliest documentations of the Singapore Sling was not until 1930, when it was listed in *The Savoy Cocktail Book* with the instructions: ¼ lemon juice; ¼ dry gin and ½ cherry brandy to be shaken, strained into a glass and topped with soda water.

In Charles H Baker Jr.'s *Around the World With Jigger, Beaker and Flask*, he encounters many a sling, including the Singapore Gin Sling, which he dubs "a delicious, slow-acting, insidious thing"; the Raffles Gin Sling; and simply a Gin Sling. Across Singapore, different venues served varying gin slings, including ingredients like cherry brandy, lime juice and bitters. It's also worth theorizing that the cocktail may have originally been called the Straits Sling — Straits being the colonial name for Singapore — before its name change in the 1920s.

The most well known version of the Singapore Sling became popular at Raffles in the 1970s, and the International Bartender's Association (IBA) lists the ingredients as: 30ml gin; 15ml cherry liqueur; 7.5ml triple sec; 7.5ml benedictine; 120ml fresh pineapple juice; 15ml fresh lime juice; 10ml grenadine syrup and a dash of aromatic bitters.

Crawley's Imperial Shaker

An Eco Solution

ecoSPIRITS is the groundbreaking technology launched by Proof & Company that positively impacts both the environment and the bar industry. Developed and designed in Singapore and now rolling out globally, ecoSPIRITS is the first technology of its kind, designed to end single-use glass. Producing one glass spirit bottle creates around 550 grams of carbon emissions, and approximately 40 billion bottles are made yearly. Recycling is an imperfect solution, as it requires energy and a large percentage of glass goes to landfill.

ecoSPIRITS come in a reusable 4.5-liter vessel called an ecoTOTE. At the ecoPLANT, spirits are processed from a distillery's bulk containers into ecoTOTES, which are then sent to bars, where bartenders will fill their own bottles using the ecoTOTES. When they're empty, the ecoTOTES are sent back to the ecoPLANT for refilling. There, they are cleaned, sanitized, refilled and re-fitted with tamper-proof sealing, ready to be distributed again.

In 2019, Raffles reopened after a restoration, bringing with it an updated Singapore Sling created under the guidance of Proof & Company. The updated drink uses Cherry Sangue Morlacco, Ferrand Dry Curacao and Luxardo Maraschino cherries as well as ingredients made especially for the Singapore Sling, including London dry gin Widges, developed by Proof's own Jason Williams, with notes of juniper, cardamom and sweet orange. Scrappy's Bitters also created a Spice Plantation blend, inspired by the spice plantations of old Singapore, using botanicals such as nutmeg, mace and cloves. Respected Australian bartender Jason Crawley created Crawley's Singapore Sling Grenadine using pomegranates, cane sugar and natural red coloring to give the Singapore Sling its iconic hue.

This updated Singapore Sling is a climate-friendly cocktail, owing to the fact that the gin, cherry brandy and curacao are delivered to Raffles in ecoSPIRITS' ecoTOTES to reduce single-use glass and carbon footprint. The maraschino cherries and bitters are also shipped in bulk format, meaning thousands of kilograms in packaging waste is eliminated annually. Besides reducing waste, under the ecoSPIRITS Forest Program, the hotel plants one native tree in the Kalimantan or Sumatran rainforest for every ecoTOTE delivered to the hotel.

The Singapore Sling is undoubtedly a tourist favorite; a must-have for those wanting a refresher to beat the tropical humidity of the Lion City in the colonial surrounds of Raffles, throwing peanut shells on the floor of Long Bar. So much so, that you can imagine all that shaking can tire out bartenders. To combat this, the Long Bar has a Crawley's Imperial Shaker atop the bar to shake the cocktails manually at high volume with a crank handle. And you'd be quite right in assuming the shaker comes from the aforementioned Jason Crawley, who reproduced this piece of 200-year old machinery originally known as an Imperial Shaker Machine.

Singapore Sling

This drink is the updated and current version of Asia's globally recognized classic cocktail.

30ml	Widges Gin
15ml	Benedictine
10ml	Luxardo Sangue Morlacco
10ml	Ferrand Dry Curacao
60ml	fresh pineapple juice
20ml	fresh lime juice
10ml	Crawley's Singapore Sling Grenadi
1 dash	Scrappy's Spice Plantation Bitters

Method
1. Place all ingredients into tins with ice and shake.
2. Strain over cubed ice into a hurricane glass.

Garnish
Pineapple wedge and cherry

SLEEPLESS DAWN

by Aki Wang for Indulge Experimental Bistro, Taipei

Aki Wang has earned himself the title of the godfather of Taipei cocktail culture, and with good reason. He opened Indulge Experimental Bistro in the capital of Taiwan over a decade ago, when the cocktail scene was still nascent. Bars at the time barely knew the classics, and used imported alcohol and ingredients, whereas Aki was showcasing the best of Taipei.

Aki wanted to introduce Taiwanese flavors and products through his cocktail creations, and was one of the first bartenders to blend tea drinking culture with cocktails. In-depth research into how best to preserve the fragrance of tea when blending with alcohol, and the foraging of local ingredients, are what set Aki and Indulge apart.

Taipei's locale near both mountains and sea allows Aki to access quality ingredients. He forages in the mountains for tea and herbs, and signature cocktail Sleepless Dawn is Aki's story of the connection between himself, Taiwan and Taipei — all captured in a dawn-like drink.

"Taiwan is a unique island in the heart of Asia and one of the most beautiful and attractive places in the world, with a landscape covered by six types of unique and rare vegetation. It's also surrounded by modern architecture as well as nature, combining the old and new," Aki explains. He goes on to share that Taiwan's distinct seasons and 24 solar terms — an ancient Chinese calendar divided into 24 segments based on the movement of the sun to guide farming — are the inspiration for his creativity.

His reason for calling the cocktail Sleepless Dawn: Taipei is a city that never sleeps. "Also, one of the city's famous spots is Elephant Mountain, and the best time to visit is around 4am to 5am. From downtown, it only takes 20 minutes to get there and after just 30 minutes of climbing, you are rewarded with the most beautiful scenery. I've lived in Japan, Poland, London and New York, but for me, Taipei will always be the most beautiful city and I still want to make cocktails to tell its story."

The presentation and garnishes of Sleepless Dawn represent Taipei's natural environments: succulent plants for the mountain; the color to represent the light of dawn; the ice cube for clouds. Wild ingredients that can be foraged are portrayed in the gin and the aroma of the unique teas, and the flowers and herbs used are those that can be found in the city.

Sleepless Dawn

The Sleepless Dawn is Aki's homage to his home of Taipei, and its diverse landscape and beauty.

125ml	assorted infusion*
50ml	The Botanist Gin

Method
1. Shake ingredients with ice.
2. Fine strain into a chilled stemless wine glass.

Garnish
Fresh succulent plants

*Assorted infusion
500ml of 40% ABV neutral spirit; 750ml water; 125g fresh gardenia; 82.5g limnophila aromatica; 750ml baozhong tea syrup**
Blend all ingredients in heavy-duty blender. Place blended mix in rotary evaporator flask and set to following specs until original liquid has evaporated: temperature 70° C; rotation 85rpm; pressure 300mbar; condenser temperature -10° C. Cut ABV to 40%. Combine 750ml baozhong tea syrup; 335g assorted infusion; 7g succinic acid. Mix all ingredients and store at room temperature.

**Baozhong tea syrup
1.5l water; 90g of 20% fermented and 10% roasted baozhong tea; 375g caster sugar
Brew tea with sugar for 15min, then strain and chill to room temperature.

SMOKY HUNTER

by Gagan Gurung for Tell Camellia, Hong Kong

Tea cocktail bar Tell Camellia takes its name from the Camellia Sinensis plant, an evergreen bush whose leaves are used to produce tea. At the helm is Gagan Gurung, serving up a menu of cocktails using teas from around the globe.

Born and raised in Nepal, Gagan has had a connection to tea ever since he was a child. Growing up, he visited lots of tea

plantations, sampling their products and fostering a lifelong love for tea. When Gagan moved to Hong Kong, he originally wanted to be a chef, but after a year on the job, he wanted more interaction with guests, and so he pursued bartending instead.

Gagan had always wanted to open a bar that embodied his childhood and motherland, and figured a tea-driven concept represented not only Nepal, but most of Asia as well. And so, Tell Camellia was born.

Tell Camellia's Teatails center around a tea's country of origin. Take the eponymously named Australia, which features a blend of whisky, Yalangi Rain tea, blue cheese, clarified strawberry, eucalyptus, and Tim Tams (an Aussie snack favorite). Meanwhile, tea twists on classics use base spirits redistilled with tea, like a redistilled cold brew oolong bourbon that stars in the Oolong Old Fashioned. Of course, there's also a Teapresso Martini on the menu, featuring roasted green tea vodka, malted cocoa and pistachio dust.

The redistilling technique — using the bar's in-house rotary evaporator — also redistills gins with a variety of teas to create Tell Camellia's range of T-Tonics, from refreshing Kyoho grape to smoky lapsang souchong.

The bar also hosts regular tea and cocktail workshops, educating guests on teas and how to pair them with spirits. Some of Gurung's favorite teas are white teas, for their floral and honey notes as well as their high-antioxidant health benefits. "I love to blend white tea with vodka to create amazing twists on classics like cosmopolitans and vodka martinis," says Gurung. "The vodka absorbs the tea's tannins and honey flavors, giving the vodka a new character and aroma."

He's also a fan of lapsang souchong: "It's so unique, and great to drink after dinner. The black tea smoked with pine wood gives a really nice smoky aroma, which is perfect for warming you up in winter. It also goes really well with gin, almost giving the gin aged characteristics in color and aroma as it becomes woody and almost peaty, which makes for a perfect smoky Gibson or gin sour."

Gagan says tequila and jasmine green tea make a perfect pairing, as tequila's distinct earthy and fruity aromas are heavenly when infused with jasmine green tea. "As the green tea is mixed with jasmine buds, it creates floral and grassy notes that perfectly complement tequila."

Dark-roasted oolong has a burnt toffee aroma and depth, which is a no-brainer to match with the toasty, sweet caramel aroma and flavor of bourbon. Gagan says one of the bar's best-selling cocktails is the Oolong Old Fashioned. Meanwhile, rum pairs well with both Pu'er or darjeeling. "Due to the earthiness and slightly woody, wet forest aroma of Pu'er, it works really well with dark rum. Darjeeling tea works well with light rum thanks to its unique fresh and fruity aroma, and it makes for an amazing daiquiri."

Smoky Hunter

Gagan believes amaro and bitter cocktails are a growing trend in Hong Kong; he was inspired by guests looking for both a strong tea and a bitter flavor profile.

45ml	lapsang souchong-infused Fernet Hunter*
15ml	chestnut liqueur
4 dashes	cassia bark tincture**
2 dashes	saline solution^

Method
1. Stir all ingredients in a mixing glass with ice.
2. Serve over a block of rock ice into a rocks glass.

Garnish
Lemon twist

*Lapsang souchong-infused Fernet Hunter
10g lapsang souchong tea; 700ml Fernet Hunter
Mix tea leaves with Fernet Hunter. Refrigerate for at least 2hrs.

**Cassia bark tincture
5g cassia bark; 200ml vodka
Mix together and vacuum seal for 12hrs at room temperature. Strain and bottle.

SOUTH CHINA ICED TEA

by Yao Lu for The Union Trading Company, Shanghai

S hanghai-born, Texas-raised Yao Lu took a similar career path to many in the industry, getting behind the bar when the hotel he worked at was short-staffed. The difference was in what made him fall in love with the job.

While studying hospitality at the University of Houston, hoping to get on the corporate hotel path, Yao took a job as a room service waiter at a hotel in the Texas Medical Center. A self-proclaimed impressionable young man, he was curious about bartending — and wanted better tips — so he took a job at the bar.

Due to its location, the hotel guests were medical staff from all over America, as were the patients and their families. "A majority of my guests were going through terrible things and it created a dark environment, but it was crucial to shaping who I am, and it taught me a lot about empathy," says Yao.

One story he recalls is when he served a guest whose husband and three sons were all getting chemotherapy, and with not much else to do, the woman frequented the bar's happy hour, sitting quietly in the corner. "I made it my mission to cheer her up," shares Yao. "I tried to make her smile for at least five seconds to make that day five seconds better than the day before."

Yao clowned around the bar and eventually the woman warmed up to him and the pair struck up a conversation. "A part of me is happy when I see others happy, and that's when I realized bartending was way beyond making drinks. It's you at the front line feeling all the raw emotions of the guests. As a bartender, you have the power to steer them to a happier place."

Wanting to further his skills, after many applications and rejections, Yao finally landed a job at Anvil Bar and Refuge by renowned Texan bartender Bobby Heugel. With experience under his belt, Yao later moved back to Shanghai and tended bar in the city for a few years before opening The Union Trading Company with his partner and chef, the late Austin Hu in 2014. May he rest in peace.

Union brings American hospitality to China to create a warm, neighborhood bar vibe that makes everyone feel welcome. Union was one of the first bars I visited in Shanghai, and that night was pivotal in so many ways.

Firstly, it was the first trip my best friend Beckaly Franks and I took together, as she was guest bartending at Union — she also got a bar full of strangers to sing happy birthday to me when the clock struck midnight on my 29th birthday. It was also of course where I met Yao, who has become a very dear friend. And most importantly, it's where Beckaly introduced me to Theo Watt, founder of DRiNK Magazine. At around 2am and many cocktails in, I told Theo how much I loved his magazine and would love to work for them. Fast forward a year, and I was, and this really kick started my career in the bar industry. It's also worth noting that Yao had connected with Theo online prior to moving to Shanghai, and it was Theo who sweet-talked Yao into moving back.

South China Iced Tea

Yao's Chinese rift on the classic whisky sour features tea and homemade kumquat marmalade.

25ml	blended Scotch whisky
30ml	strong lapsang souchong tea
22.5ml	fresh lemon juice
15ml	honey
1 tbsp	kumquat marmalade*

Method
1. Put all ingredients and ice into a tin and shake.
2. Strain into a porcelain tea cup on cubed ice.

Garnish
Candied kumquat and a rosemary sprig

*Kumquat marmalade
900g kumquat; 1.4kg sugar; 250ml water
Rinse kumquats; cut in half and remove seeds. Place in food processor; process until coarsely chopped. On stove, place pot, combine kumquats and water. Bring to full rolling boil over high heat, stirring constantly. Stir in sugar; return to full rolling boil. Boil and stir 1min. Remove from heat; skim off foam. Let cool.

SPEAK LOW

by Shingo Gokan for Speak Low, Shanghai

As a teenager growing up in Tokyo, Shingo Gokan was on the path to take over his father's business. At 18, Shingo began seeking a part time job in bars and kitchens and landed a job at a high-volume, 100-seater restaurant bar. While he wanted to learn a skill, bartending was never meant to be a serious job. Twenty years later, he is one of the world's most renowned and awarded bartenders.

Aged 23, he moved to New York, still planning to eventually return to Japan and lead his father's company. He applied for a job at speakeasy Angel's Share, but was rejected for his lack of visa and fluency in English. Shingo took a job in another restaurant bar, where he learned English by memorizing whole sentences like a script. Six months later, Angel's Share took him on, and he eventually became the head bartender and bar manager.

It wasn't until six years in, when Shingo won the Bacardi Legacy cocktail competition in 2012, that his career took off and he realized bartending was the path he wanted to follow.

Winning the competition gave him the opportunity to travel while guest bartending all over the world, meaning he met new people, learned new skills and discovered new cultures. The first time he participated in the competition was also when he met his friend and future business partner Steve Schneider, principle bartender of the legendary Employees Only in New York and its sister venue in Singapore. The pair later went on to open The Odd Couple in Shanghai in 2019.

In 2014, Shingo opened his first bar, Speak Low, in Shanghai. The bar was inspired by Shingo's time at Angel's Share, and improved upon what he believed was not a sustainable model. "Angel's Share was always so busy, and every day from 6pm, we had a queue of guests outside and were full until we closed," he explains. "Angel's Share had lots of rules, including having to be seated, and in groups of no more than four people, in a venue of only 50 seats. We also only had one bar station to serve these 50 guests and it became very difficult. I couldn't make room at the bar for friends or overseas bartenders who visited, and I couldn't really serve the cocktails that I truly wanted to."

Shingo says Speak Low is his translation of Angel's Share, divided across four levels. Hidden behind a ground floor bar tool shop facade, the bar's second floor is a casual, American-style high-volume spot; the third floor is the area for Shingo to create the drinks he'd always wanted: a quality space to share his talents; while the top floor is a special space for visiting friends and family.

This three-in-one bar concept became Shingo's signature, and he followed up with Sober Company in Shanghai, and The SG Club in Tokyo. Over the years, Shingo has expanded the SG Group empire to nine bars of varying concepts, a bar tools and glassware company, and a shochu brand, winning several awards for both his bars and personal achievements.

Whenever I speak with Shingo, I'm always floored by how down to earth and creative he is. I ask him how he does it all and he credits his team, a staff that grew from 10 at Speak Low to now over 120 across the group, for helping to support and develop his ideas. "Traveling is also one of my biggest inspirations and because I'm not always behind the bar, I have some time to read, watch movies and learn new skills. Even as a kid I was always creating new things — I didn't like following rules," says Shingo.

Speak Low

Speak Low is Shingo's winning Bacardi Legacy drink that earned him global recognition and inspired the name of his first bar, while showcasing Japanese ingredients matcha and yuzu.

30ml	white rum
30ml	Bacardi Reserva Ocho
15ml	Pedro Ximenez sherry
1 tsp	matcha powder

Method
1. Put all ingredients and ice into a tin and shake.
2. Strain into a chilled rocks glass with a large ice cube.
3. Zest a yuzu rind over the drink to express oil.

SUJEONGGWA

by Bannie Kang

Bannie Kang is arguably one of the most **humble, high-achieving** bartenders in Asia. Originally from Korea, Bannie moved to Singapore in 2010, where she worked at Swissotel The Stamford's back of house due to her lack of English. She was eventually transferred to City Space bar as a cocktail waitress, where she toyed with the idea of becoming a bartender, but her limited English hindered interactions with guests.

She returned to Korea, working part time in a coffee shop, studying English and taking part in a training program learning basic classic cocktails and spirits knowledge. Feeling better equipped, she returned to City Space bar as a waitress again, sometimes jumping behind the stick to make drinks. Upon entering her first cocktail competition, the Diageo World Class 2013, she ranked in Singapore's top four and was promoted to bartender.

Bannie reveals she loved competitions as a young bartender, saying they made her feel more independent and responsible for her own development. She eventually moved to Anti:dote, where her manager and mentor Tom Hogan actively encouraged her to speak to guests to help develop her language and hospitality skills.

Bannie entered Diageo World Class again in 2014, determined to win; she made the Singapore finals, but decided it was time to get some other competition experience under her belt. In 2016, she made the global finals of the Bacardi Legacy and in 2017, she won the global finals of the Black Cow Golden Top Cup 2017. She went on to achieve her dream of winning the Diageo World Class Bartender of the Year in 2019, and later opened the since-closed MU in Taipei.

Now back in Singapore, Bannie and her chef husband Tryson Quek host a private cocktail and tasting kitchen called Sidedoor from their home, hoping to expand to a brick and mortar space soon.

Bannie has become a good friend of mine over the years, and I'm always inspired by how she can smash her goals yet remain one of the sweetest and kindest people in the business — which she insists she'll never leave as she's so passionate about making people happy.

Sujeonggwa

Bannie's twist on the classic Sazerac shows off her roots by taking inspiration from a Korean cinnamon punch of the same name, which Koreans drink during Mid-Autumn Festival.

50ml	peanut butter-infused cognac*
10ml	sujeonggwa syrup**
2 dashes	walnut bitters
1 spray	absinthe

Method

1. Add all ingredients into an ice-cold mixing glass with ice and stir for approximately 15 seconds.
2. Strain into a Nick and Nora glass over a large ice sphere.
3. Spray absinthe over the drink.

Garnish

Bamboo leaf

*Peanut butter-infused cognac

200g peanut butter; 1l frozen cognac
Add peanut butter into frozen cognac and infuse for 24hrs, then fine strain before use.

**Sujeonggwa syrup:

1l water; 100g chopped red dates;
50g thinly sliced ginger; 25g cinnamon;
5g osmanthus; 300g honey; 10g maple syrup
Soak chopped red dates in hot water 15min before use.
Boil water and add ginger, cinnamon and osmanthus.
Simmer for 30min. Remove pot from heat and add honey
and maple syrup. Leave pot to cool, then strain.

T & T

Cross Yu

L ike many bartenders, Shanghai bar legend Cross Yu began as a server, fascinated by the bartenders at the restaurant where he took his first hospitality job. With no formal training available, Cross's quest to tend bar led him to a hotel. Underqualified, he ended up working anywhere but behind the stick.

In 2006, he scored some much-needed cocktail training at the now-closed Laris, joining the team and kickstarting his bartending and cocktail competition career. Fast forward eight years, and Cross took the leap to open his own bar, E.P.I.C, in 2014. That year, bars such as Shingo Gokan's Speak Low and Yao Lu's The Union Trading Company also opened, and along with E.P.I.C, these bars really put the wind in the sails of Shanghai's bar scene.

Located in Shanghai's French Concession, in a narrow building spread over three floors, E.P.I.C,

Cross Yu (front) and Teddy Tang (front left)

much like Cross himself, is no stranger to awards. The bar's brand of familial, laidback hospitality is paired with one of the best playlists in Asia plus quirky cocktails. Every detail is a culmination of experience gained from and lessons learned at Cross's previous jobs.

The music, predominantly disco and funk, is particularly noteworthy here. Cross regards it as paramount to the bar experience, saying it can make or break a venue and guests' evenings, as ultimately it's a large part of a bar's vibe.

Cross also went on to co-found Charcohol and open multi-concept venue Glory, but it's E.P.I.C that is Cross's crowning jewel. The establishment gained international attention after smashing onto The World's 50 Best Bars list in 2021. "Do epic shit!" is the bar's modus operandi, and Cross is definitely a purveyor of epic-ness.

T&T

E.P.I.C's bar manager Teddy Tang was inspired one day while eating teriyaki chicken and drinking Thai tea. Wanting to replicate those flavors in a cocktail, she scoured her fridge, only to find Sichuan beef paste. Thanks to Peddlers' use of Chinese spices like Sichuan pepper, it was the obvious spirit choice, paired with coconut syrup for a Southeast Asian flavor.

30ml	beef paste-infused Peddlers Gin*
15ml	white rum
30ml	Thai tea
20ml	lime juice
22ml	coconut syrup

Method
1. Shake all the ingredients with ice.
2. Fine-strain into a Collins glass with cube ice and top with crushed ice.

Garnish
Shredded chili pepper, orchid and pandan leaf

*Beefpaste-infused Peddlers Gin
75g beef paste; 750ml Peddlers Gin
Mix beef paste with gin in vacuum seal bag. Sous vide mixture at 65°C for 1hr. Cool to room temperature in freezer for at least 24hrs. Remove solid part and filter liquid part with coffee filter paper in fridge or at cool temperature (in case oil melts again).

THE CIGAR VENDING MACHINE

by Summer Chen for Vender, Tainan

Taiwanese Summer Chen moved to study in Singapore at the tender age of 19. She took a bartending job for extra cash, before deciding to stick with it and stay in Singapore to further her craft. Her tenure in the city saw her crowned Global Champion of the 2018 Gin Mare Mediterranean Inspirations competition in Ibiza, and the following year she was declared the Global Champion of the 2019 Bartenders Society World Finals in Paris.

Summer has since returned to her native Taiwan to open Vender in Tainan with her partner Darren Liu. Their goal is to deliver a great experience to guests through drinks and bartending, in a bar styled on a vending machine. Based on the premise that vending machines are everywhere, providing essentials to keep you going throughout the day, Vender serves great drinks to get a night going or to cap off a great evening.

Summer Chen (front right)

To enter Vender, one must open the vending machine entrance by inserting a coin to unlock the door. Of course, the bar also houses actual vending machines. One sells bottled cocktails and beers, and the other is a capsule dispenser. Inside every capsule is an unknown cocktail, so guests can choose their drink at random, without knowing what it is beforehand.

Vender's interactive cocktail menu features 12 pockets representing Vender's 12 signature cocktails, with each pocket containing the main ingredients used in the drink. Guests are encouraged to touch, taste, smell and explore each individual ingredient to gain a better understanding of the cocktails, guided by information in the menu detailing the taste profile. Each drink is named after different types of vending machines and features various herbs and spices from Southeast Asia.

Summer stays true to her bartending roots with a nod to Singapore, by including lots of cultural elements like local foods bak ku teh (a Hokkien pork rib broth) and chili crab on the food menu. But what would a homage to Singapore be without the Singapore Sling? Vender's welcome drink includes a shot of the infamous cocktail, whose history is detailed in this book, using freshly made grenadine, house-infused cherry brandy and Taiwanese pineapples.

The Cigar Vending Machine

Vender's bestseller uses Southeast Asian spices to bring out unique flavors reminiscent of smoking a cigar, inspired by Summer and Darren's first foray into Cuban cigars and old Cuban rum.

50ml	dark rum
15ml	red wine syrup*
20ml	fresh lemon juice
30ml	egg white
10ml	aromatized wine
3 dashes	chocolate bitters
Handful	Taiwanese cypress wood chip

Method

1. Put all ingredients into a shaker and dry shake, before adding ice and shaking again.

2. Strain into a rocks glass.

3. Cover the glass with a glass dome and usin a smoke gun, burn the cypress wood chips and inject the smoke into the dome.

*Red wine syrup

1l red wine; 30g cinnamon; 15g star anise; 6g cloves; 10g orange peels; 10g lemon peels; sugar

In a pot over high heat, boil red wine until all alcohol evaporates. Switch to low heat and add remaining ingredients and simmer for 15min. Remove all solids ar strain red wine into measuring jug. Measure total amou of red wine and add in equal parts sugar. Boil mixture ov high heat and stir until all sugar has dissolved.

THE GREEN FIELDS

by Deepak Koranga at The Bombay Canteen, Mumbai

Restaurant and bar The Bombay Canteen shakes up classic cocktails reimagined with Indian flavors. Founded by Sameer Seth and Yash Bhanage, The Bombay Canteen is surrounded by the old and new of Mumbai — the old mill structures and new glass office buildings of Kamala Mills.

Drinks here pay tribute to the untold stories of Mumbai through creatively crafted menus that tell these tales, from a pop-up art book celebrating Mumbai's Art Deco architecture, to a calendar inspired by the slang and colors of the city streets. There was even a menu in the style of a historical guidebook of the golden age of the cinematic "Talkies" talking film, since cinema is wildly popular in India. Drinks also take inspiration from the kitchen's culinary ethos, using local and seasonal ingredients to create housemade infusions, bitters, shrubs and tonics.

ak Koranga (fourth from left) and team

The Bombay Canteen has its own sourcing consultant to help the bar and restaurant work with the best local and indigenious ingredients from farms in Maharashtra and beyond, all to support small-scale producers and to source directly from them.

The Green Fields cocktail, created by assistant bar manager Deepak Koranga, has grown to be a crowd favorite at The Bombay Canteen. Each cocktail on the Art Deco menu drew inspiration from the most iconic buildings in Mumbai, conveyed through color, form and association.

The Green Fields building in south Mumbai is unlike other Art Deco buildings in the city. It is very distinct, standing out due to its light green color, so of course, the drink is green in hue thanks to the green tea component. Light and creamy with floral notes, the glassware is also selected to elevate the appearance of the theme, so The Green Fields is served in a coupe glass, reminiscent of the building's curved windows.

The Green Fields

This drink, from the bar's first menu and inspired by The Green Fields building in Mumbai, remains ever-popular.

45ml	gin
30ml	jasmine and green tea syrup*
30ml	lime juice
20ml	egg white

Method
1. Put all the ingredients into a shaker and dry shake to get the desired texture.
2. Add ice to the tins and shake again.
3. Fine strain into a coupe glass over ice.

Garnish
Slice of starfruit

*Jasmine and green tea syrup
100g jasmine flowers; 4 tsp green tea leaves; 1l 1:1 sugar syrup^
Add jasmine flowers and green tea leaves to sugar syrup. Infuse for 12hrs and strain.

THE
HOBNAIL

by Beckaly Franks for The Pontiac, Hong Kong

When The Pontiac opened its doors in 2015, it was touted as an American-style neighborhood dive bar, but it has evolved into so much more over the years. The bar comes from the discoball brain of Beckaly Franks — a force to be reckoned with in the bar community — who now manages late night dinner and dancing spot Quality Goods Club. The Pontiac's 'We don't give a fuck' attitude has won the hearts of many, and the bar has become a beacon of inclusivity and a go-to for the LGBTIQ+ community.

Led by powerhouse Jen Queen and an all-female team, the dark but inviting bar is a mishmash of bras and feather boas hanging from the rafters, punctuated by a rocking soundtrack ranging from heavy metal to disco and everything in between. Weekdays here are perfect for parking up at the bar and chatting to the bartenders, and weekends are often a swan dive into glorious shoulder-to-shoulder chaos. Whatever day of the week, the night ends with the infamous "Midnight Special", in which the staff jump atop the bar and pour laybacks for guests to give thanks.

The Pontiac is a curious case of a bar with so much character, and yet is so hard to define, which is really the true essence of a dive bar: it's for the people. The cocktails

The Hobnail

A Pontiac stalwart that has been on the menu since day one, The Hobnail riffs off of modern classic cocktail the penicillin, dialling the ginger up to 100 for a spicy kick.

45ml	blended Scotch whisky
23ml	ginger syrup*
23ml	fresh lemon juice
5ml	Averna amaro
2 dashes	aromatic bitters

Method
1. Put all ingredients and ice into a tin and shake.
2. Strain into a chilled rocks glass with cubed ice.
3. Zest an orange rind over the drink to express oil.

Garnish
Orange twist

*Ginger syrup
500g ginger root; 700g caster sugar
Cut ginger into coin-sized chunks. Juice ginger root
slow juicer. Fine strain. Combine 150g sugar to 100
ginger extract and blend until sugar dissolves.

here are far from dive bar standards, however. Beckaly's The Hobnail became an instant classic at the bar, and The Pontiac's menu, much like the bar, is without definition, ranging from outrageously colored slushies, to cocktails incorporating local snake wine.

The Pontiac has become a second home for many, and it's one of the first bars that I was happy to rock up to alone, knowing there would always be someone to chat to. Beckaly has become a voice and mentor for many in the industry, myself included. I'm lucky to call her my best friend and our motto in life and work is to "juice the lemons", meaning you have to do the hard yards before you can start making magic — as in, you have to prep at a bar juicing citrus before you can make cocktails! Beckaly was also a huge factor in me pursuing a career in the bar industry, which is something I'll forever be grateful for.

THE
PEOPLE'S TEA

by the team at 28 HongKong Street, Singapore

Often regarded as one of the bars that kick-started Singapore and Asia's craft cocktail revolution, 28 HongKong Street celebrated a decade of service in 2021. Founders and New York drinking buddies Spencer Forhart, Paul Gabie and Snehal Patel moved to Singapore, and when they couldn't find the elevated drinking dens they'd become accustomed to, they decided to build their own.

The unassuming shophouse facade with no signage gives way to a bar hidden in plain sight. Inside, the venue touts familial hospitality, a curated playlist bolstered by a great soundsystem, and cheeky drinks with names like Lethal Weapon, made from tequila, falernum, togarashi, shio koji lime, sesame and cucumber.

28 HongKong Street is the kind of bar where anything goes. A chilled evening parked at the bar indulging in good chat and American comfort food could very possibly morph into a wild night of pumping tunes and rattling the rafters.

The People's Tea

This cocktail is a combination of two classic and beloved whisky drinking traditions: the Japanese whisky highball, and the Singaporean whisky and green tea.

35ml	genmaicha-infused Japanese whisky*
2 dashes	saline solution^
25ml	acid-adjusted umeshu**
90ml	soda water

Method

1. Add all ingredients except soda to a chilled highball glass.

2. Fill glass with a clear-cut ice spear or the largest cubes available.

3. Top up with soda water and gently mix to combine.

4. Zest a lemon rind over the drink to express oil

Garnish
Nori chip

*Genmaicha-infused Japanese whisky
600g Japanese whisky (single grain preferred);
12g loose-leaf genmaicha tea
Combine tea and whisky in neutral container and leave to steep at room temperature for 25min. After steeping, strain through paper coffee filter. Once strained, store at room temperature for up to 1mo.

**Acid-adjusted umeshu
600g umeshu; 6g citric acid powder;
3g acid phosphate (optional)
Combine acids and umeshu in container and stir to dissolve. Once dissolved, store in refrigerator for up to 1mo.

28 HongKong Street took the number one spot at the inaugural Asia's 50 Best Bars in 2016, and many notable bar personalities have worked here, before going on to open their own venues. The success of the bar also led the founders to create Proof & Company, a spirits distribution company-turned-consultancy responsible for assisting in the conceptualization of some of Asia's best bars — a few of which feature in this book.

I have been fortunate enough to be allowed behind the stick at this institution as part of a guest bartending shift as well as a cocktail competition. Both were definitely the kind of nights where anything goes: swinging from the ladders propped on the back bar and ruckus good times!

THEOBROMA

by Shuzo Nagumo for Memento Mori, Tokyo

Shuzo Nagumo, the man behind several Tokyo bars, made a name for himself at the diminutive Mixology Salon, his eight-seater bar in Tokyo's Ginza Six shopping mall. The bar specializes in "teatails" — cocktails incorporating various kinds of tea including hojicha, oolong and gyokuro. Teas are infused in-house in spirits, and feature varieties such as soba cha vodka, hojicha bourbon, sencha gin and oolong rum. The bar also uses lesser known teas, such as Uva black tea, which has a menthol flavor.

Tea twists on classics include the Green Tea Old Fashioned, which can be sampled via a tasting menu or on its own.

One of Mixology Salon's signatures is the Hoji Cozy: hojicha dark rum, cacao liquor, homemade vanilla syrup and hojicha powder served in a matcha bowl.

Speaking of cacao, Shuzo's Memento Mori is a cacao-focused cocktail concept, where cocktails use all of the components of cacao, including the pulp, nib, husk and butter. These are then combined with various botanicals such as fruits, flowers, plants, roots and seeds. In true Shuzo style, there's also a selection of cacao tea cocktails, using cacao spirits and cacao tea as well as a selection of dishes that incorporate cacao.

Theobroma is the scientific name for cacao, and also the name of one of Memento Mori's signatures. Shuzo wanted to create a martini or Manhattan-like drink using cacao, and he describes the cocktail as like a cacao soup. "Cacao, like coffee, varies in taste depending on the place of origin, variety and how long it is roasted for," he says. "Depending on what kind of cacao you choose, the taste will be different, and you'll never taste the same two cacaos again."

Theobroma

This is a spirit- and cacao-forward cocktail with a flavor profile that can change dramatically depending on the variety of cacao nibs used.

30ml	cacao nib-infused vodka*
15ml	cacao nib-infused rum*
10ml	vintage port
2.5ml	creme de cassis

Method
1. Put all ingredients into a wine glass and mix well.
2. Pour into a mixing glass with ice and stir about 40 times.
3. Strain into a cocktail glass.

*Cacao nib-infused vodka and rum
210g cacao nibs; 700ml vodka/rum
Infuse in a container for 2wks at room temperature. Fine strain and bottle. Place in a freezer for over 24hrs. Ready to use when cacao fat and fine powder settle at bottom of bottle and upper part of liquid becomes clear.

TIGER'S EAR

by Niks Anuman-Rajadhon for Asia Today, Bangkok

Niks Anuman-Rajadhon is renowned in the Bangkok bar scene. With three bars in Chinatown, he first opened Teens of Thailand in 2016. The small 20-seater has a huge collection of gin and specializes in gin and tonics, with twists such as Thai tea G&Ts. Along with The Bamboo Bar, Teens of Thailand gave rise to the cocktail scene in the country's capital.

Niks and his partners followed up a year later with Asia Today: a bar with eclectic decor such as a pink neon sign stating "This bar is better than Teens of Thailand", and a huge plastic shark dangling from the ceiling. Asia Today works with foraged ingredients, as well as ones they grow themselves and source through local producers. Wild honey is a big focus here, with the bar housing a huge collection.

This love for honey is perfectly captured in the Eastern Honey Bee, made with Old Tom gin; wild Apis cerana honey; and lime topped with a wild honey foam; all served in a beeswax mug.

Alcohol laws are strict in Thailand, meaning advertising and pre-batching drinks; infusing and barrel-aging spirits; and using modern culinary equipment now popularly employed in bars such as a rotary evaporator, are all illegal. Alcohol bans during the COVID-19 pandemic made it hard for bars to survive, and Niks led the charge, campaigning against these laws as well as other restrictions with fellow industry folk.

Another bar of his, Tax, features rough-and-ready decor with controversial artwork, and specializes in vinegars that don't contain alcohol — meaning Niks can make them himself, taking advantage of a loophole and continuing to pave the road to defiance.

Tiger's Ear

Asia Today focuses on local produce, and tiger's ear leaf is something Niks ate a lot of in Chiang Mai, admiring its taste and strength as a plant that can grow anywhere. He first tried it in a drink in the form of a gin and tonic, which also inspired this highball-style cocktail.

30ml	dry vermouth
15ml	London dry gin
3ml	Thai garlic brine
15ml	local wild honey (preferably Apis cerana)
17ml	fresh lime juice
3 dashes	aromatic bitters
90ml	soda water

Method
1. Add all ingredients except soda to tins a shake with ice.
2. Fine strain into an ice-filled highball gla
3. Top with soda and stir gently.

Garnish
Tiger's ear leaf

TOMATO

by Tokki Soju Hospitality for Tokki Bar, Seoul

Housed on the fourth floor of the RYSE Hotel — a sister hotel to the ACE Hotel in Los Angeles — Tokki Bar is located in the Seoul party district of Hongdae. The bar is a project from the team behind Tokki Soju and is an homage to the quintessential Brooklyn neighborhood cocktail bar.

Five members of the Tokki team met while living in New York City, where the Tokki distillery was originally based, and wanted to incorporate those founding roots into this venue. All alcohol is made in-house from the spirits, liqueurs, bitters and beer, and there's a hearty menu of Italian American favorites on offer too.

Tokki Bar's drinks are made with spirits that were created by the Tokki Soju team, whether that's Tokki Soju Gold Label, Tokki Soju Black Label, Sŏnbi Gin or Sŏnbi Vodka. The cocktails are created using different techniques, from milk punches and infusions to carbonation, adding nitrogen and the like.

Besides the cocktails, Tokki Bar also creates a rotating collaboration beer, made in partnership with different local breweries.

Twist on a Classic

American Brandon Hill moved to Korea in 2011 in a quest to study Korean fermentation practices, taking his learnings back to New York with him. He was approached by a Korean restaurant to create a high quality traditional soju, and so Tokki Soju — tokki means rabbit in Korean and 2011 was the year of the rabbit — was born. Hill moved back to Korea and Tokki Soju is now produced in Chungju.

Tokki Soju uses ingredients including fermented sticky rice sourced locally, as well as wild fermentation starter nuruk and reverse-osmosis filtered water. Instead of using a vacuum still, Tokki Soju produces its soju using a copper still. The distillery produces Tokki Soju Black, White and the aged Gold varieties, as well as Sŏnbi gin and vodka.

One of the cocktails on the menu, The Milk Punch Curry, features Tokki Bar's in-house curry cordial, made using lemongrass syrup, ginger, lime leaf, pandan, curry powder, milk, coconut cream and citrus stock, blended with Sŏnbi Gin and coconut water.

Credit has to be given to Tokki Soju, who are changing perceptions beyond the mass-produced green-bottle soju and defining the new category of craft soju. Green-bottle soju is essentially ethanol and added sweeteners, but craft distillers like Tokki Soju cook the rice, ferment and distill, harkening back to more traditional methods.

As I used to live in Korea, I have fallen victim to the crippling hangovers of over-consuming green-bottle soju. It may be cheaper than water in Korea, but you pay the price the next day! I even got to a point where I had to initiate a self-imposed soju ban for my own good, but the rise of new craft brands is definitely helping me appreciate the category on a whole new level.

Tomato

Inspired by the sweet, sour and refreshing natur of a paloma cocktail, but with an additional umami flavor profile. The clarified drink is also intended to surprise and excite people, as it's clear, not red like a tomato.

10ml	Sŏnbi Gin
10ml	Sŏnbi Vodka
15ml	acid solution*
20ml	lemongrass syrup**
Top up	force-carbonated clarified tomato water***
1 dash	saline solution^

Method
1. Add everything except the force-carbonated tomato water into a Collins glass.
2. Fill with ice, top off with force-carbonated tomato water, and stir.

*Acid solution
1l water; 50g sugar; 30g citric acid; 20g malic acid; 10g tartaric acid
Mix until dissolved.

**Lemongrass syrup
1l water; 100g lemongrass; 1kg sugar
Put lemongrass and water in pan and bring to boil. Turn o heat and leave to rest for 20min. Filter out lemongrass an pour in sugar and stir until dissolved.

***Force-carbonated clarified tomato water
2l tomato juice; 15g of pectinase
Mix together, then refrigerate overnight. Filter through coffee filter. To force-carbonate, use PET bottle and carbonator cap, with CO_2 regulator set to 58PSI.

TRIGONA
OLD FASHIONED

by the team at Bar Trigona, Kuala Lumpur

Bar Trigona is a beacon of sustainability, celebrating the rich produce of Malaysia. Housed in the Four Seasons Kuala Lumpur, the bar takes its name from a stingless bee called the trigona, which produces a unique, citrusy honey.

When the bar's concept was being conceived, the Bar Trigona team traveled around peninsular Malaysia, discovering ingredients, exploring tea plantations and visiting the indigenous Orang Asli people, the oldest inhabitants of the peninsula. Just 45 minutes outside of the city, they came across Dino's Trigona Honey Farm. Run by Dino Kelulut, the farm is operated out of his backyard, and the story inspired the team to build their concept around this unique honey, using it in many of their cocktails.

Bar Trigona also operates an Adopt A Hive program, through which

adopters' funds help to support, protect and grow bee populations; educate young apiarists and equip them with beekeeping skills; as well as contribute to establishing more bee sanctuaries.

Bees aside, Bar Trigona showcases local fruits and producers, and minimizes waste by upcycling ingredient scraps, limiting packaging from suppliers, and ordering in bulk. You won't find plastic straws, sachets, coasters or napkins here, and the bar also has a rotating menu of special cocktails whose sales contribute to planting fruit trees locally. Proceeds from the cocktails go to Bar Trigona's long-time collaborator Ong Ning-Geng, cacao farmer and owner of Chocolate Concierge, who is responsible for planting and tending to the farm.

The bar has been recognized for its dedication to sustainability, and it would be remiss to not mention Ashish Sharma, the ex-bar manager of Bar Trigona. In his tenure, the bar was the first in Malaysia to feature on The World's 50 Best Bars list in 2020, and won the Sustainable Bar award for two years running. Ashish is now working on the sunny shores of Miami, and though he has departed, his team continues his dedication to local produce and the environment. While he'll be missed, I have fond memories of times spent tasting local honey flights at the bar or visiting Ong's farm with Ashish, harvesting fresh cacao and durian and tasting them straight from the tree.

Trigona Old Fashioned

Bar Trigona's take on a classic Old Fashioned uses local trigona honey, which the bar is named after.

55ml	bourbon
5ml	Cynar
5ml	trigona honey
2 dashes	Orleans bitters
1 spray	cedarwood essential oil

Method
1. Put all ingredients into a mixing glass with ice and stir.
2. Strain into a rocks glass over a large ice cube.

Garnish
Cube of honeycomb

UKIYOE SOUR

by Hiroyasu Kayama for Bar Benfiddich, Tokyo

Bar Benfiddich, helmed by maestro Hiroyasu Kayama, could be confused for an ancient apothecary. Kayama-san doesn't just create cocktails — he harvests the ingredients used in them from his family farm in Chichibu, an hour from Tokyo. You'll often find him behind the bar, donning his white jacket with a suribachi and surikogi (a Japanese pestle and mortar) in hand, exuding the sort of elegance Japanese bartenders are known for.

This modern-day "doctor" takes his inspiration from medical books that date back over a century, researching flavors, botanicals and recipes. There's no menu here, and bartenders will ask your preferences before whipping something up.

Concoctions are therefore varied and many, including homemade Italian-style bitters made to order, bison grass vodka, gentian liqueur and fresh fruits to complement base spirits and more. If your drink is to include a sweet element, you might even see Kayama-san pressing fresh sugar cane or creating highballs using tonics and sodas made with botanicals from his farm.

While no-menu bars are de rigueur in Japan, Bar Benfiddich stands out for its innovation, use of fresh ingredients and in-house fermentations and liqueurs. Many Japanese bars don't tend to work with homemade ingredients, so Bar Benfiddich breaks the mold with what could be called a farm-to-glass concept.

My first visit to Bar Benfiddich was a healing one. My husband and I spent our first Christmas together in Japan, landing in Tokyo first. Just before arrival, I was struck down with a stuffy head cold, losing my sense of taste and smell but not wanting to miss out on great cocktail experiences. I told Kayama-san I was under the weather, and please could he make something to cure me. Instead of a hot toddy, he made a kind of toddy and Moscow Mule hybrid with plenty of Japanese whisky, ginger and mystery herbs. Watching him work was something to behold — he was somewhere in between bartender, pharmacist and wizard. Whatever he concocted, it cured me and the fiery ginger helped restore my senses.

Ukiyoe Sour

The Ukiyoe Sour is a Japanese take on a pisco sour, using purely Japanese ingredients and spirits. Ukiyo-E (meaning pictures of the floating world) is a genre of art that was of great importance in Japan's Tokugawa period (1603–1867).

60ml	junmai daiginjo sake
20ml	potato shochu
20ml	yuzu juice
2 tsp	wasanbon (Japanese sugar)
1	egg white

Method
1. Dry shake all ingredients in a tin.
2. Then add ice and shake again.
3. Strain into a wooden box.

Garnish
Hinoki leaf or rosemary and a dash of umami bitters*

*Umami bitters
100ml vodka; 3g bonito flakes
Infuse bonito flakes in vodka for 1wk.
Strain and put in bitters bottle.

WELCOME TO THE JUNGLE

by the team at Tropic City, Bangkok

The clue is in the name of this jungle hideout in the middle of Thailand's sprawling capital of Bangkok. Swedish hospitality veterans Philip Stefanescu and Sebastian De La Cruz are the brains behind the bar. Along with their team, they're expert hosts, rum lovers and purveyors of good times.

The neighborhood bar is tucked down an alley in the creative district of Charoenkrung, and is hard to miss, thanks to a mural of bright green parrots and neon flamingo-shaped lights. Stepping into this tropical den inspired by the Caribbean, South Pacific, Southeast Asia and beyond, really is transportive in a city like Bangkok.

Colorful decor matches the vivid drinks, which make use of

Sebastian De La Cruz (left) and Philip Stefanescu

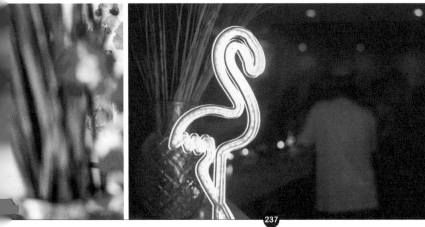

techniques such as fat-washing and clarification; and ingredients like high quality fruits, vegetables, herbs and spices from Thailand and Southeast Asia. While the cocktails aren't all rum-based, the bar also hosts regular rum tastings. Rum flights allow drinkers to sample five rums of varying styles and historic backgrounds.

Tiki drinks aren't the sole name of the game here, but Welcome To The Jungle — one of the very first cocktails crafted at Tropic City that's featured on the signature cocktail menu ever since — is without a doubt a tiki take. Using Pattawia pineapples from Chaiyaphum province in central northeast Thailand, the drink is served in a hollowed-out pineapple which, let's be honest, everyone wants in a tropical bar.

Tropic City very nearly caused me to miss a flight home, while I was there for the closing party of the BKK Bar Show. I had stupidly booked a flight departing first thing in the morning and had to reluctantly drag myself away from the throwdown. I don't think I've made the rookie error of booking a crack-of-dawn flight since!

Welcome to the Jungle

This tiki tipple combines various flavors and multiple spirits to create a unique complexity that has proven to be a very popular crowd-pleaser since Tropic City opened its doors.

20ml	dark rum
20ml	white rum
10ml	apricot liqueur
10ml	allspice dram
20ml	vanilla syrup*
25ml	fresh pineapple juice
25ml	fresh orange juice
30ml	fresh lime juice

Method
1. Put all ingredients into a shaker and shake with crushed ice until cold.
2. Strain into a hollowed-out pineapple or a brandy glass.
3. Top the drink with fresh crushed ice.

Garnish
Dehydrated orange wheel, orchid flower, pineapple leaf, umbrella pick

*Vanilla syrup
650ml water; 1kg sugar; 1 vanilla pod
Heat all ingredients on medium heat until sugar dissolved. Let cool, bottle and store in fridge.

XOI MIT

by Dinh Thep for Stir, Ho Chi Minh City

S tir in southern Vietnam's Ho Chi Minh City is helmed by award-winning bartenders Lam Duc Anh and Dinh Thep. It's one of the first in a new wave of independently owned bars, as Vietnam's cocktail scene takes flight.

The name, of course, comes from the basic bartending technique — a simple skill that's hard to master. Lam also says the verb describes many daily activities in Vietnamese life, like the Vietnamese coffee with condensed milk that you need to stir before enjoying, or a kitchen technique like the stir-fry.

Lam was originally studying to be an English teacher when he took extra jobs to support his family. He eventually fell in love with

Dinh Thep (center) and team

bartending, meeting new people and being rewarded by delighted guests. Dinh was relatively new to the industry, and he and Lam met during various competitions and guest shifts, before eventually deciding to partner up.

Hidden up some stairs opposite Ben Thanh Market — a hugely popular tourist spot — the speakeasy-style jazz and blues bar serves cocktails with Vietnamese names, inspired by the country's fantastic street food and drink culture. The cocktail ingredients are mostly local, but some are seasonal and regional. The team spent a lot of time, effort and calories researching local street food and drink, basing drinks off of dishes such as the dau hu nuoc dua (warm soft tofu with ginger and brown sugar). Twists on classics include the Banh Da Colada with rum, local rice wine, coconut, pineapple and homemade baby-corn cordial.

The team also scoured history to research the concept, taking inspiration from Ho Chi Minh City's golden era: 1960s to 1970s Saigon, as the city was formerly known. The result is a bar with Indochine glam and a fully Vietnamese menu, team and decor. Stir waves the flag for the Southeast Asian country's flourishing cocktail scene.

Xoi Mit

Xoi Mit is inspired by the Vietnamese breakfast of the same name, consisting of sticky rice with jackfruit.

45ml	blended Scotch whisky
45ml	jackfruit cordial*
100ml	soda water

Method

1. Stir the Scotch and jackfruit cordial with ic
2. Pour into a highball glass over ice.
3. Top up with soda water.

*Jackfruit cordial

500g of fresh jackfruit; 10g pandan leaves; 1l water; 7g citric acid; 7g tartaric acid; 8 buds jasmine flower

Sous vide jackfruit and pandan leaves in water at 60° for 2hrs. Cool down to room temperature, then strain clarify through coffee filter. Add citric and tartaric aci and stir well until dissolved. Add jasmine flower buds liquid and refrigerate to infuse for 4hrs.

LE THANH TON
THÀNH TÔN

ZIPPY ZIPPY CHEERS

by Karl Too for Happy Stan, Kuala Lumpur

Happy Stan is a Kuala Lumpur coffee cocktail concept named after Pulitzer Prize-winning travel writer Stanton Delaplane, who is credited as the man who introduced the Irish Coffee to the US. In 1952, Delaplane met Jack Koeppler, owner of The Buena Vista in San Francisco, and Koeppler asked Delaplane to help him recreate the Irish Coffee, which was served at Ireland's Shannon Airport.

The pair set about perfecting the recipe throughout the night, and their biggest challenge was getting the cream to float on top of the coffee. Despite all the caffeine, the pair worked so hard that legend has it Delaplane almost passed out by the end.

Koeppler was extremely dedicated, and even jetted to Shannon Airport to sample the original for himself. On return, he visited San Francisco's dairy-owner mayor, who determined that the cream needed to be aged for 48 hours to achieve an exact consistency to stay afloat.

The Buena Vista still remains one of the most famous spots for Irish Coffee, and this origin story inspired Happy Stan owner Karl Too to create a concept that he says synchronizes the skills of both bartenders and baristas by serving coffee, cocktails and coffee cocktails. Of course, Happy Stan has its own Irish Coffee, using Indonesian cold brew. Other coffee cocktails include the classic espresso martini, the coffee Negroni and the Zippy Zippy Cheers: a Negroni twist using local ingredients.

Happy Stan also serves twists on other classic coffee cocktails, such as the cheekily named Not Cafe Brulot — a twist on the Cafe Brulot, if that wasn't obvious — with dark roast coffee, cognac, triple sec, cinnamon, cloves and lemon peel served hot. There are also simpler serves, such as the Mr Black Cold Brew Coffee Liqueur and tonic, for when you need a caffeine boost without getting too boozy.

Zippy Zippy Cheers

The Zippy Zippy Cheers is a Negroni twist incorporating Malaysian ingredients like torch ginger flower, and laksa leaves that you can find in asam laksa (one of Malaysia's famous dishes). Karl has dedicated this drink to the country's bartenders.

25ml	Mr Black Cold Brew Coffee Liqueur
20ml	torch ginger flower and laksa leaves bianco vermouth*
20ml	3-year-old umeshu
10ml	Italian bitter bianco aperitif

Garnish
Orange peel-wrapped maraschino cherry

Method
1. Pour all ingredients into a mixing glass with ice and stir.
2. Fine strain over a large ice cube in a doubl rocks glass.

***Torch ginger flower and
laksa leaves bianco vermouth**
16g fresh laksa leaves; 16g fresh torch ginger flower;
750ml bianco vermouth
Clean and trim fresh torch ginger flower and laksa leaves. Measure and place in sous vide bag. Sous vide at 51° C for 2hrs. Place in ice bath then discard all solids. Keep refrigerated.

#STILLHURTING

by David Ong for The Curator Coffee and Cocktails, Manila

David Ong (leftmost, behind the bar)

David Ong is one of the pioneers of Manila's bar scene, which really kicked off when his first bar The Curator Coffee and Cocktails opened.

The bar found life with humble beginnings, tucked behind a sublet wine store. Stripping the walls to bare cement and adding in a bar and communal tables, the windowless and signless space was ready to serve. The venue was at least in a good location, on a street packed with bars and restaurants.

It wasn't until three years later that the coffee part of The Curator came into play, when David took over the wine store, making it a daytime coffee shop — and birthing the coffee by day, cocktails by night concept of The Curator. After another three years, enjoying immense success that also saw David touring on guest bar shifts and earning a reputation as a party starter, he followed up with OTO in a gentrifying neighborhood once known for its red light district and what David calls "crazy happenings".

Opening the bar with his music-loving school friends, the music-driven concept, named after the Japanese word for sound, boasts an extensive vinyl collection and solid soundsystem. Decked out in plywood to improve acoustics, the bar attracts music lovers from all walks of life, but is known for David's party-throwing antics. To give you an idea of just how well-watered David likes to keep his guests, he's known for dishing out ABC shots — a killer combo of absinthe, Bacardi 151 and Chartreuse — something he used to drink during university, after pre-drinking at home. The shots then became a practical joke with bar industry friends.

"The Curator is definitely more prim and proper," laughs David. "We use a lot of equipment, like a rotary evaporator, centrifuge and spinzall. This allows us to prepare more in advance and focus on hospitality as well as serving great cocktails." OTO's drinks are mostly well-executed classics using some homemade ingredients, and is a good starting point for those finding their feet in the world of cocktails.

David's love of coffee doesn't end at The Curator. He also founded EDSA Beverage Design Group, which sources coffee, has a lab to produce sodas, ginger beer, kombucha, cocktails, distillates and more, and also features roastery #YKWRoasters.

#StillHurting

In David's own words, this drink is sweet at first, but with a bitterly beautiful ending — like a painful love that contributes to the creation of poetry, power ballads, soap operas and Rachel McAdams movies.

30ml	Patrón Reposado Tequila
30ml	coffee-infused vermouth*
15ml	espadin mezcal
15ml	Campari
2 dashes	Xocolatl Mole Bitters
2 dashes	orange bitters

Method
1. Build and stir in a mixing glass.
2. Strain into a rocks glass over ice.

Garnish
Orange peel

*Coffee-infused vermouth
1 part espresso blend coffee grounds to
10 parts sweet vermouth
Flash-infuse coffee grounds with sweet vermouth in whipped cream dispenser with nitrogen charger, fo 5min. Strain through paper filter and store in chiller.

250

GLOSSARY

The following recipes, terms and spirits were mentioned throughout the book.

Saline Solution

4 parts hot water; 1 part sea salt

Blend until dissolved.

Sugar Syrup

1:1 sugar syrup:

1 part hot water;
1 part caster sugar
(or rock sugar, agave, honey etc.)

Blend until dissolved. Keep refrigerated.

2:1 sugar syrup:

1 part hot water; 2 parts caster sugar (or rock sugar, agave, honey etc.)

Blend until dissolved. Keep refrigerated.

TERMS

Shake

Place all ingredients into a cocktail shaker tin with plenty of ice. Seal with the other tin, ensuring they are closed tightly. With one hand placed firmly at either end of the tins, shake vigorously for approximately 20 seconds, until the outside of the tins frost up. Break the seal of the tins to open.

Dry shake

Shaking method without ice, used in cocktails with egg whites to emulsify and build body or froth in a cocktail. Shake for around 10 seconds. Usually followed by a wet shake as above.

Stir

Using a mixing glass and bar spoon, stir ingredients with ice for around 20 to 25 seconds.

Fine Strain

Straining the drink from the tins or mixing glass using both a Hawthorne strainer and fine strainer to catch shards of ice and fruit pulp. Also known as double strain.

Build

Adding each ingredient one by one into a glass.

Throw/Roll

Used to both chill and aerate a cocktail and combine thicker ingredients together. Using a Boston shaker, fill one half with ice and trap it down with a Hawthorne strainer. Slowly pour the liquids between the tin halves five to six times.

Zest

To gently squeeze a citrus rind to express oil.

Muddle

To slightly crush ingredients in a tin with a muddler to release aromas.

Rotary Evaporator

Piece of equipment used in modern bartending for distillation or redistilling.

Hawthorne Strainer

A strainer with coils and perforated holes designed to keep ice and other large ingredients in the tins when straining.

Cobbler Shaker

Three-piece shaker with main body and two lids, with a built-in strainer.

Boston Shaker

Two-piece shaker, most commonly used.

Centrifuge

Piece of equipment used in modern bartending to clarify liquid by spinning at high speed, causing the molecules to separate and the sediment to settle at the bottom.

Caviar Box

Allows precision sphere-making in cooking and bartending.

Aquarium Aerator

Adds air bubbles into liquid to create foam-like bubbles.

SPIRITS

Batavia Arrack

A sugarcane and red rice spirit originating from Indonesia, distilled in a pot still.

Makgeolli

An alcoholic fermented Korean rice wine.

Baijiu

A Chinese spirit made from fermented sorghum, with 12 different variations.

Shochu

A Japanese spirit distilled from rice, barley or sweet potatoes.

Soju

A Korean spirit made from rice, wheat, barley, potato or sweet potato.

Umeshu

A Japanese plum liqueur.

GLOSSARY

REFERENCES

PEOPLE

Kim Choong | Jason Williams | Shingo Gokan | Charlene Dawes | Antonio Lai | Beckaly Franks | Jen Queen | Tom Egerton | Jay Khan | Lorenzo Antinori | John Nugent | Agung Prabowo | Kenzo Lee | Jesse Vida | Vijay Mudaliar | Bastien Ciocca | Andrew Ho | Joshua Ivanovic | Keith Motsi | Indra Kantono | Gan Guoyi | Sam Jevons | Natalie Lau | Julia Mellor | Arkadiusz Rybak | Simone Rossi | Gagan Gurung | Tiana Ludhani | Max Traverse | Sandeep Kumar | Jesse Vida | Colin Chia | Shelley Tai | Juan Yi Jun | Jessica Hutchinson | Jay Gray | Andy Loudon | Rusty Cerven | Aki Wang | Angus Zhou | Summer Chen | Cross Yu | Yao Lu | Lolita Goh | Jamie Rhind | Niks Anuman-Rajadhon | Ronnaporn Kanivichaporn | Emma Thompson | Julian Brigget | Ashish Sharma | CK Khoo | Karl Too | Hidetsugu Ueno | Shuzo Nagumo | Hiroyasu Kayama | Phil Abowd | Demie Kim | Terry Kim | Diane Kang | Minakshi Singh | Arijit Bose | Yash Bhanage | Lam Duong | Lam Duc Anh | Vu Ngoc | David Kaye | David Ong | Kalel Demetrio | Kiki Moka | Bannie Kang

WEBSITES

Finding the creator of Jungle Bird (thirstmag.com)
The icy side of Hong Kong history (bbc.com)
Ice House - 2nd location [1862-1955] (gwulo.com)
Bamboo Cocktail (everythinginthebar.blogspot.com)
Tokugawa Period and Meiji Restoration (history.com)
drinkmagazine.asia

PHOTO CREDITS

Potato Head: All Is Amazing

BOOKS

Baker, Charles H., The Gentleman's Companion: Complete edition.
Echo Point Books & Media. 2015. Print edition.
MacElhone, Harry, Harry's ABC of Mixing Cocktails. Souvenir Press. 2011. Print edition.
Craddock, Harry, The Savoy Cocktail Book. Girard and Stewart. 2015. Print edition.
Poister, John J., The New American Bartender's Guide. Signet. 1999. Print edition.
Berry, Jeff, Intoxica. SLG Publishing. 2003. Print edition.
Boothby, William, The World's Drinks and How to Mix Them. Chump Change.
1907. Print edition.
Uyeda, Kazuo, Cocktail Techniques. Mud Puddle Books. 2010. Print edition.

BRANDS

Thank you to the following brands for their support: Sông Cái
Distillery, ecoSPIRITS, Nusa Caña, Peddlers, Campari, Mr Black
Coffee Liqueur, Tokki Soju, Citadelle, Plantation, Beam Suntory,
Monin, Nikka, Patrón, Flor de Caña, Fernet Hunter, Lyre's,
The Botanist and Cointreau.

REFERENCES

ABOUT THE AUTHOR

Cocktails of Asia is bars, spirits and cocktails expert Holly Graham's first book. She is the Managing Editor (International) of DRiNK Magazine, Asia's leading bar industry platform. She has featured on the Bar World 100: a list of the world's most influential figures in the bar industry, since 2020, as well as on Tatler's Asia's Most Influential: The Tastemakers List 2021.

Holly is also an Academy Chair for The World's 50 Best Bars and Asia's 50 Best Bars and sits on both the education and Spirited Awards committees for Tales of the Cocktail. Holly has judged several renowned cocktail and spirits competitions around the world. She is also the founder of the Asia Women In Booze community for women in the alcohol industry, and successfully organized Speed Rack Asia 2019, an all-female speed bartending competition that raises money for breast cancer charities.

Holly was previously the Food and Drink Editor of Time Out Hong Kong, and cut her teeth bartending at The Old Man Hong Kong, during which time the bar was ranked number one on Asia's 50 Best Bars 2019.

Published in Hong Kong
Printed in China

ISBN 978-988-77560-6-4

ManMoMedia

manmomedia.com